Improve your ENGLISH

ENGLISH
in EVERYDAY LIFE

Stephen E. Brown and Ceil Lucas

D0452136

New York   Chicago   San Francisco   Lisbon   London   Madrid   Mexico City
Milan   New Delhi   San Juan   Seoul   Singapore   Sydney   Toronto

1 2 3 4 5 6 7 8 9 10 11 12 13 14 15 16 17 18 19   DOC/DOC   0 9 8

ISBN   978-0-07-149717-6 (book and DVD)
MHID   0-07-149717-X (book and DVD)

ISBN   978-0-07-149721-3 (book alone)
MHID   0-07-149721-8 (book alone)

Library of Congress Control Number: 2007941299

McGraw-Hill books are available at special quantity discounts to use as premiums and sales promotions or for use in corporate training programs. To contact a representative, please visit the Contact Us pages at www.mhprofessional.com.

Note: Views expressed in the DVD are those of the interviewees and do not necessarily reflect the views of the authors/editors or the publisher.

Also in this series:

Improve Your English: English in the Workplace
Improve Your American English Accent

This book is printed on acid-free paper.

May 2009

CONTENTS

INTRODUCTION

English in Everyday Life consists of eighty-four interview segments with everyday people, not actors, speaking English in the United States. The interviews are organized into ten chapters. Each chapter focuses on a different aspect of everyday life, from the family and the home to free time, sports, food, and the use of language. The goal in using an interview format was to elicit natural speech and to allow the speakers to express themselves as freely and naturally as possible. In these interviews, you will hear the vocabulary and sentence structures that real speakers use to talk about their everyday lives.

Because we wanted to provide learners of English with natural models of spoken English in the United States, those being interviewed did not memorize or rehearse their remarks. You will meet people of all ages and nationalities, from all walks of life: a policeman, a nurse, accountants, a paramedic, students, teachers, a librarian, a mechanic, a government worker, an IT professional, a travel agent, a sign language interpreter, musicians, and others.

Each chapter includes the complete transcript of each interview segment as well as definitions of vocabulary words, idioms, and constructions whose meanings or cultural references may not be immediately obvious to a nonnative English speaker. You will find questions and exercises at the end of each chapter that are relevant to both the text of the interview and your own personal experiences. We recommend that you consult a comprehensive American English dictionary in conjunction with the use of the DVD and workbook.

ABOUT THE TRANSCRIPTS

What you will hear on the DVD and see in the transcripts are examples of actual speech. Our goal is to provide examples of English as it is spoken by a wide range of people in the United States today. You will hear speakers from many states—Maryland, New Jersey, Massachusetts, Arkansas, Illinois, Maine, Minnesota, and Michigan—as well as speakers from Canada, India, Guyana, England, New Zealand, Cameroon, Egypt, and Spain. Also, you will hear one speaker whose speech has many features of what is known as African-American Vernacular English (AAVE). So you will hear English spoken with many different accents. You will also see a deaf user of American Sign Language (ASL) with her interpreter.

You will notice that while all of the speakers are fluent, they sometimes use what some consider nonstandard or even ungrammatical forms of English. And you will see that not only do the nonnative speakers use these forms but native speakers of American English frequently use them as well. Some of these speakers are very fluent users of varieties of English used in other countries, such as India, varieties that have been referred to as "World Englishes" and that differ from American or British English in very systematic and nonrandom ways.

You will notice that when people speak, it is not at all like a newscast being read by an anchorperson on the evening news or like the written language that you might see in textbooks. You will see that people don't always speak in complete sentences—they hesitate; they interrupt themselves; they correct themselves; they start one sentence, give it up, and go on with another one. While the speakers clearly knew that they were being filmed, what you see and hear is, for the most part, very natural speech. Our goal was to reflect this naturalness in the transcripts. Interjections and discourse markers such as *um, uh,* or *er* appear throughout the interviews and are transcribed exactly as they are spoken. Sometimes people talk at the same time, which is indicated in the transcripts by brackets around the simultaneous speech.

The transcripts also reflect the use of many customary and idiomatic constructions found in American English: *take it up a notch, so-and-so, such and such, like, y'know, c'mon, gonna, wanna,* and many others. Notes explaining such constructions appear at the end of each chapter.

It is our hope that you will find these materials innovative and useful for learning English as it is used in America today.

How to Use These Materials in the Classroom

The DVD and workbook of *English in Everyday Life* have been designed for use in any classroom, laboratory, or home setting. These materials, which are suitable for high school classes, university courses, and adult education programs, can be used as the second semester of an elementary course.

The way that language is used by speakers in these materials can serve as the basis both for in-class discussions and for homework assignments.

The DVD and the workbook provide eighty-four segments, which should be used as follows:

1. Select the segment to be used and simply *listen* to it, *before* reading the transcript of the segment. The student can do this on his or her own or as part of a class activity.

2. After listening to the segment, *read* and *discuss* the transcript carefully, making sure that all of the vocabulary words and structures are understood.
3. Then, *listen* to the segment again, this time using the transcript. Students may want to listen to the segment several times at this point.
4. In the classroom, answer and discuss the questions about both the segment and the students' experiences. And, of course, these questions and exercises can be assigned for homework.

Outlining a Course by DVD Segment

The instructor can decide how many segments to cover per week. Eighty-four DVD segments allow you to use the DVD and the workbook for an entire academic year. And the flexibility of the materials allows you to pick and choose the order in which to present the material. Each segment on the DVD is numbered on the menu and in the text so that you can pick exactly which one you want to focus on.

Sample Lesson Plan: One Week
First Day: Listen to the selected segments perhaps two or three times in class (do not read the transcript at this point).

Second Day: Read the transcripts out loud, making sure that the students understand all of the grammatical constructions, vocabulary words, and cultural references.

Third Day: Listen to the segments again, first without the transcript and then with the transcript.

Fourth Day: Discuss the transcript and the DVD segment and answer the questions pertaining to the segment. Assign as homework the questions and exercises that pertain to the students.

Fifth Day: Go over the questions and exercises pertaining to the students. Ask them to read their answers aloud, and have the class ask additional questions.

The DVD segments and their transcripts can very easily be supplemented with materials that relate to the topic of the segment. For example, the segments on Food can be supplemented with menus or recipes. The important thing is to be creative and to get the students involved.

Additional Activities

1. Ask the students to summarize in writing and also aloud what is said in a given segment.
2. Ask the students to write the question that leads to the speaker's response. Also, ask them to write additional questions to be asked.
3. Have the students interview one another on the topic of the segment in front of the class:
   - Help the students write their interview questions.
   - If possible, record these interviews on audiotape or miniDV. Listen to or view the interviews and discuss them as a group.
   - Have the students transcribe these interviews, complete with hesitations, self-corrections, and so forth. Make copies of the transcript for the other students. The teacher may review the transcript but should make corrections only to errors in transcription—in other words, if the speaker uses a nonstandard form and the student transcribes it accurately, you should not note it as an error. This is a good opportunity to point out the differences between spoken language and written language.

- Have the students write questions about their transcripts, similar to the ones in the text.
- Have the students record an interview with a native or fluent speaker, based on one of the DVD topics, and follow the same procedures just listed. Help the students prepare their questions, review the transcripts, and share them with the class. Also, ask the students to write questions to accompany their transcripts.

ACKNOWLEDGMENTS

We are very grateful to Patrick Harris for his excellent work filming and editing the DVDs. We thank all of the people who were willing to be interviewed and Holly McGuire, Christopher Brown, and Julia Anderson Bauer of McGraw-Hill Professional; Jim Dellon, Ivey Wallace, and Jayne McKenzie of Gallaudet University; Kevin Keegan of Hubert Blake High School in Silver Spring, Maryland; Mike Solano and Merchant's Tire in Laurel, Maryland; and Jim Smith, Kim MacKenzie Smith, and The Skydivin' Place in Kingsdale, Pennsylvania.

CHAPTER 1

LIFE IN AMERICA

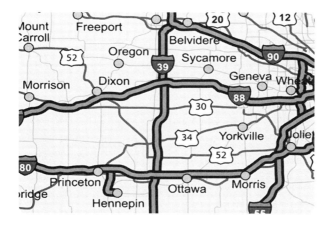

In this chapter, interviewees talk about various aspects of life in the United States and how life in the United States may differ from life in their countries of origin.

1. DRIVING ACROSS AMERICA

MAN: I have driven throughout most of the country. Um, so, there's, you know, the speed limits, well, it's fifty-five, uh, there're . . . Do you know how the ro—, the roads—by the way, this is fascinating—do you know how the road systems are laid out in the, in the U.S.? Do you know that? They're laid out, uh, if you, if you know locally where we are here, um, 95 is the main route. Ninety-five goes from the northern tip of Maine down to the southern tip of Florida, which is the entire **Eastern Seaboard**. If-if the, if the country were a rectangle, which it pretty much is, the, all **interstates** ending in odd numbers—95, 85, 75, 65, 55, going all the way up to I-5—I-5 runs the northern tip of Washington to the southern tip of ⌈California⌉.

WOMAN: ⌊San Diego.⌋

MAN: All-all the way down the West Coast, so you have the, you know, 95 'n 5 to 95 and going West Coast, you have, uh, 10, which runs through Texas and all the way across there to the northern tip, which is 100, I think, and that runs through North Dakota, so, uh, a college friend of mine, on our first venture out, decided we were, we live on, sorta in the middle, which happens to be 70, it's not quite 50 but a little bit farther north and 70 runs all the way across from, you know, Maryland all the way to California, um, and, uh, we decided we were going to do 70 on 70—miles per hour, that is—80 on 80, 90 on 90, and 100 on 100! And we did it. So we-we were cruisin' across country in that manner and I've been th—, I c—, I would say I've been through at least half of the states. And if you drive through Kansas, the first five miles is pretty much exactly the same as the next five hundred-plus miles that you have got to travel to get across it. It's a very long state.

2. WHAT DO YOU LIKE ABOUT AMERICA?

WOMAN: It was the most interesting thing to me, the **change of the seasons**. I think that is just absolutely . . .

'**cause** I guess as I grew up with just one season. In fact, I shouldn't say one—two seasons: we have the wet season and the rainy season. But it's summer all year-round. And I just love especially fall. I'm a fall person. I just love, I love to see the colors, the trees when they, oh, turn those beautiful colors—that's really, that's what I like about . . . And what I like, too, television, ooh, I'm a television nut. I look at television all the time. And in Guyana, we don't see the kind of programs that you have here, so . . .

INTERVIEWER: So what do you watch?

WOMAN: I like crime stories and, like "Law and Order" and, in fact, I watch all "Criminal Intent," all of those "Law and Orders."

INTERVIEWER: And what else?

WOMAN: I like game shows, too. I love "Jeopardy"; I love "Jeopardy." Uh, yeah, game shows and "Law and Order," those are my, crime stories, I like things like that.

Well, as I mentioned, the seasons. We don't have spring, summer, autumn, winter. We have summer all year-round.

INTERVIEWER: Right.

WOMAN: Um, another thing, the traffic here. You just have to contend here with cars and maybe couple bicycles. But in Guyana, you've got to contend with not only the cars, pedestrians, bicyclists, we—most people ride a bicycle in Guyana, they-they don't drive, they ride a bicycle. And there's also something we call a donkey cart, which is something like a **flat-bed truck**, but instead of bein' pulled by a-a car like in front, it's pulled by a donkey. And they're also, they also have the right of way, too, on the streets, too. So that's-that's something; every time I go home, I keep wondering, "How did I ever drive in Guyana before?" because I know for sure I can't drive there now, so . . .

3. AN ISLAND IN MAINE

WOMAN: Taiwanese, both parents are from Taiwan, came to the States for graduate school, uh, and then decided to stay both for political reasons and for career reasons. Um, uh, my parents came through, their Ellis Island was Kansas, uh, Univer[sity of Kansas] at Lawrence.

INTERVIEWER: [Kansas.]

WOMAN: Middle of, middle of the country, that was, I guess they were pulling a lot of Taiwanese students at that time so they came through there for their graduate school and then a job opportunity opened in Maine so that's-that's how the family ended up being the only Taiwanese family within a hundred-mile radius in Maine.

INTERVIEWER: When did your parents come to the U.S.?

WOMAN: Um, in the '60s, the early '60s.

INTERVIEWER: So how was life—have they talked about how life was different there versus life here in the U.S.— have they told you much about that or commented on that or . . . ?

WOMAN: I think it wasn't so much how life, there-there were some aspects of life that were different in the U.S. versus in Taiwan, but I think a lot of the quality of life that we had or a lot of the specifics of, uh, our lifestyle had to do with living on an island in Maine as opposed to so much being in the U.S. I don't, I wouldn't, I'm old enough now that I think I didn't have a typical **upbring-ing**, I didn't live in a typical American town. It was just so much smaller but at the same time it was inundated every summer by millions of tourists from all over the world, so we-we lived in a sort of interesting balance between being a super-super isolated small town, middle of nowhere, no traffic lights on the entire island existence, and then having this center of, uh, the **spotlight** world destination for vacationers, um, which is an interesting mix. It was, the island is sort of split into two. I lived on what they called the quiet side of the island, the western side, so that wasn't developed as a tourist destination until the last decade. Um, the eastern side is where Bar Harbor is, all these sort of big tourist areas so that was, that's always been a big tourist destination since, you know, from the last century in the 1800s. Um, so we could always in some sense retreat back to our quiet side of the island, and it-it wasn't crazy the whole summer, thanks to that. But y-you could still feel a palpable difference between the way that life was in the summer and the way that it was in the rest of the year.

INTERVIEWER: Did you enjoy living on the quieter side?

WOMAN: I did. I'm glad I lived on the quiet side. It's a little bit crazy with all the tourists.

4. WEST VS. EAST

[Note: in this segment, you hear the voice of the interviewer asking a question and then the voice of the sign language interpreter, seated on the right, who is interpreting for the deaf woman, on the left, who is using **American Sign Language (ASL)**.]

INTERVIEWER: So, you've lived—I mean, you've really lived in the West—in California and in Oregon. So how is living in the East different from living in the West?

WOMAN: Right, yes, that's a good question. The West—one thing about the West that's-that's really nice is the-the outdoors. It's, uh, it's nice to be with people who enjoy going out and doing things in nature like I do. But in the East, uh, there's so much cultural diversity, I'm able to meet so many different kinds of people. There's a lot of history here, museums, things of that nature that are really nice. And if I miss the West, I can always just fly over there and spend some time there again.

5. CANADA VS. THE U.S.

WOMAN: Well, there's work. You know, to be totally honest, that's **one of the reason** I stayed here. . . .

INTERVIEWER: Oh really?

WOMAN: Is, uh, the market—especially like in the Baltimore-Washington, and the entire like **Northeast corridor**—there's just so much work for musicians, for artists, and especially this area here because there are so many like big or middle-sized cities that all want an orchestra, and that they all want arts happening in their town, so, I mean, it's, basically, one of the-the **running gag** we have among **musician** is like, you really have to **suck on your instrument** to not find work in the Washington-Baltimore area. Really, it's like, you know. And so basically, that's, uh, the main difference for me— it's that I can, like, thrive here and make a living playing the violin, which is something I would have had a very, very, very difficult time doing in Montreal, especially since I left when I was so young and never built up . . .

INTERVIEWER: Uh-hmm.

WOMAN: . . . contacts and relationships up there.

MAN: Yeah, it-it makes me think of a funny story. Um, just the American perception of artists and musicians, um. If you go to Europe or even Canada, uh, you know, and-and you tell somebody—random person that you meet on the street—"Oh, I'm a musician," they say, "Oh, that's great!" And in-in the United States oftentimes, you meet somebody on the street and you tell them that you're a musician and they say, "Oh, well, what's your **day job**?"

A funny story: I was playing a quintet—a brass quintet job, uh, this is back when I lived in Oregon—we were playing at a fund-raiser for the, uh, the Oregon Republican Party and we were playing, you know, patriotic songs and stuff like that, and we had a short break, um, in between our-our performance, and a woman who was sitting near the front, uh, took me aside and said, "Oh, that-that man over there playing the tuba, what-what's his name?" I said, "Well, his name's Richard Frazier." And she says, "Well, what-what does he do?" I said, "Uh, he plays the tuba." And she said, "Oh, well, can-can you make a living playing the tuba?" And I said, "No, ma'am. I can only make a living playing the French horn." But that's-that's the perception.

WOMAN: Yeah, I had a similar story happening to me actually not far from here, in Hagerstown. We were playing, I was playing Maryland Symphony one week and there was a donor reception after the concert and, you know, I'm chatting there with patrons and like, I guess, guild members and, you know, other people that were attending the reception and one lady comes up to me and she's like, "You know, you look so good on stage and, like, you look like you're very, very good violinist and wh-where did you go to school, how did you get so good?" And, you know, I tell her, well, you know, my entire, like, musical education: went to Peabody, took, you know, private instruction, did bachelor, master's degree with a great violin teacher, practiced ten hours a day for ten years, and-and, you know, got a bachelor's and a master's in music, and she's like, "Wow, that's great. So what do you do?" I'm like, "Well, that's what I do. I got my education in music and I play the violin." She's like, "You don't do **maths**, you didn't do science?" Like, "No." It's like, "But you can't do that! What-what-what do you mean, you-you don't do maths? You have to take maths. What's your job?" And she just would not understand that my education, my job was music and that, you know, I didn't do maths and I could still earn a living without having done maths and science, which was, at the time, very fascinating that somebody would not accept the answer that, "I'm a musician." Which is something that would never have happened to me in Montreal.

6. LIVING IN WASHINGTON

MAN: Uh, well, this is a, is a very urban environment. Um, I'm finding things from my own perspective because the United States is not urban—it's actually rural, most of it—but my, from my own perspective, this is a very much more built-up area and, um, and in that regard it's-it's different to what my-my childhood was.

INTERVIEWER: What other places have you visited in the United States or lived in the United States?

MAN: Uh, very little. It's all, it's all been here, really, in Washington.

INTERVIEWER: Oh yeah?

MAN: Yeah, it's all, it's all been, uh, my interest is-is politics and what shapes the course of countries and why people do what they do and why civilizations behave the way that they do. So this is, if you were interested in looking at that, this has got to be an interesting place in that, in that way.

7. COMING FROM SPAIN

WOMAN: Well, I think that, uh, at that time—and this was twenty years ago—um, I think that I, uh, at first I thought that, like, the family structure was very different 'cause, of course, uh, I grew up in a country where family structures are very tight and every-everything centers around the family and that has changed, too, in Spain—but you know, at my time, eh, divorce wasn't even allowed, so when I came here, that's one of the things that struck me as different from-from Spain, that the family structure was very different, was more, uh, um, well, most people I-I met had parents who-who were divorced or, and then remarried and had stepbrothers and -sisters or half-brothers and half-sisters and that was—I mean, in Spain, you never. I mean, that was such an abstract concept, something that you heard about in movies, right? Of course, now that's normal in Spain, too. So I think that's one of the things that struck me.

INTERVIEWER: What do you like about life in America?

WOMAN: Uh, well, I-I like the academic atmosphere here. Um, uh, since I teach at a university, I think I-I benefit a lot from the **academic atmosphere**. There's a lot, there's a lot of resources, uh, easy access to grants, money, even though, of course, we complain all the time, you know, that there's not enough money, not enough support, but, of course, if you compare, uh, the situation here to the situation in other countries in-in Europe, there's a lot more resources here for-for research, and, um, also I like the flexibility, the fact that, uh, people are just so free to move around. They get tired of their job, whatever, no problem—they just move to another place, uh, start another job, and I like that kind of flexibility, whereas I think in Europe in general people are more, uh, the mentality is, "OK, once you buy your house, that's where you die." You don't really move around that much.

8. TIME IN EGYPT AND AMERICA

I usually, I go in the morning. Uh, I get a lot of phone calls from **the student**. Uh, if somebody has a problem with, in any class or has a problem with a professor or has a problem in his own life, he can talk to me about it and I can explain to him what he has to do and I always let him know about the time between here and over there. Over here, the time is very, very valuable. You have to make sure, if you have a class at two o'clock, you have to be there at two o'clock exactly. If you make it five minutes before, it's OK, but do not late one more minute than the time. And back home, timing is not, no value for the times. If you have a class at two, you show up two-fifteen, at two-thirty, it's OK. But over here, when you do that, meaning you **underestimate** the professor and he will get really upset with you. So I always focus about the time because the value here, timing here is money and back home, time is, you know, we have a lot free times.

Well, the life in America is the best. America, I consider it, uh, one of the best places in the earth. I've been traveling a lot before I came to the States. I've been in England, I've been in France, I've been in Switzerland, I've been in Greece, I've been in Turkey, Czechoslovakia, Yugo-Yugoslavia—I've been traveling a lot before I come to the States. And United States one of the best because the economy is very strong and you have a lot of jobs everywhere so that is very, very important in America. Back home, unemployment is almost 25 to 50 percent. It's very hard to get a nice decent job, and if you get a nice decent job, doesn't pay you enough money to make you live really well, so, but always go back. Home is home. Always, whatever home it is, it's the best place for myself and for anybody else, but America is the best.

9. AMERICAN MEMORIES

MAN: Well, I-I grew up in England. Uh, I was born down on the south sea coast, so if you know England, right down here, maybe a hundred miles from London, uh, in a little town called Poole, *P-o-o-l-e*. Uh, and I lived in southern England until I was about twelve years old. My, uh, my father was a-a war hero in World War II in-in India, so my memories are more related to-to that. And, uh, when I was about twelve years old, my father decided that he wanted to experience the American dream, which I called the **make a buck** myth, because the myth was that we never had much money. So we arrived in New York City, came on a boat, uh, about as old as the *Titanic*, but more successful, and, uh, lived in the Bronx. So some of my earliest American memories, uh, were hot dogs, uh, the Statue of Liberty, and American kids saying, "Hey, Slimy Limey, when are you going to learn to speak English?" So English—and timing is everything because this was few years before the Beatles—and if I had only come to America after the Beatles, I would have been **cool**. Instead, I was the **geek** who couldn't speak English. Uh, well, at that age, you know, you do what your parents want you to do, so we moved to Florida, and I went to high school in Florida.

INTERVIEWER: Where in Florida?

MAN: Uh, Pompano Beach. Home of the **Bean Pickers**. This is a time when Florida had little tourists—uh, you could literally go right to the beach. Now it's all condos for miles behind the beaches, uh. So I grew up, kind of grew up there. Kind of important to me is, when I arrived in New York, I was an English kid who had never seen a **person of color** in his life—1950s England was not a **segregated society**; there were not people of color living in England. Today it's very different. So I arrive in New York City and I lived in a boys' orphanage for a year, and all of the kids in the orphanage were black and Hispanic, Puerto Rican, African-Americans, and—very powerful experience—I mean, coming from England, living in the Bronx. When I went to Florida—**racially segregated**. The railroad tracks literally divided the town. S-so those, the juxtaposition of those three experiences probably are the most important experiences in my life in terms of what I believe in.

10. COMING FROM INDIA

MAN: Uh, now when I go back for vacation to India, I see what's-what's the difference-different. I-I find everybody working in a **slow motion**. You know, you see the slow-motion movie, the hand goes slowly, but, uh, and I-I see my brothers, uh, they take life little easy. They wake up in the morning and, uh, there's a lot of help around. Somebody comes to do the dishes, somebody comes to do the laundry, and somebody else is doing the ironing, and they don't have to do anything. My, but, my brother says he's very busy—I see him doing nothing. He just-just-just goes; he doesn't even drive his own car, and, uh, his, I mean, his wife doesn't even iron the clothes. It's just waiting. He just goes for the shower; somebody comes, takes out his clothes; he changes, of course; and, uh, he goes to job. There are people who take care of the job. He's, just says, "Yes" and "No." People come to him, "Uh, this is OK?" "Yeah, OK." "Is this fine?" "OK." Accountant come and says that. He's not a big businessman—he's probably does half of the turnover that I do here—but he-he's like a king. And, uh, when I come back here, from the time I land U.S. airport, I have to pull my own bag, I have to drive my own car, I have to come home, pull my bags, take it myself in, and empty them myself. I have to do my own laundry, I have to wash, I have to clean the house myself. My, when my father came, he saw me cleaning the house, with the bathrooms. He said, "You, I thought this was America." I said, "Yeah, this is America. That's why I do it. You don't do it in India." He has never cleaned the bathroom. Somebody else does it for him. So life in India, now when I see, is like a luxury life. They think that I'm-I, since I have a little more money than them, so I'm-I have more luxury life, but unless you come and live here, uh, you realize it's-it's like super speed versus slow motion.

Doesn't give you time to think—that's good thing about, uh, life in America. When you-you grow old, you don't start, you never think you're old because you don't have time to think. And, uh, whatever you have, you have, what you don't have, you have no time to think, so time, lack of time is a blessing, in a sense. And, uh, of course I like, uh, if you, if you are enthusiastic and if your body allows you to work hard, you can open any kind of business; you don't have too much of bureaucracy, not too much of red tape, you can start business pretty quick, and, uh, of course, uh, you have liabilities, you have to work hard to do that but, uh. Yeah, you don't have to run over a period of one year, uh, like, uh, many other countries, like in India. America is very, very easy. I mean, I can just simply walk into a bank and show my good credit and take a loan for anything. I mean, I can buy a house, virtually nothing in my pocket. I can say I'm a home-owner and back home in India, I need to have at least 80 percent, so, uh, I mean, there are a lot of good things. I mean, I like, uh, I like to drive, I like to go for, uh, vaca-tion on-on, the driving. Good roads, I don't have to worry too much about it, cars are pretty good. Even if I have the best car in India, I can't drive at the speed I drive here. So there are a lot, a lot of good things. I mean, I, once I get used to, now I think now I am used to here, I cannot go back and, uh, have the slow-motion life anymore.

INTERVIEWER: Interesting.

11. CHANGING TIMES

Oh, oh, that's-that's a loaded question, you know that—seriously loaded. There was a time when-when I was growing up that, uh—and I sound like a **geezer** here—but there was a time where, you know, you didn't lock your door, um, I never had a key to my house. Those times, those-those-those ways still are out in **the West**. Uh, it-it's less gentle than it used to be and let's say, I'm not, don't even get me into why this-this could have happened.

12. SMALL-TOWN LIFE

That's an interesting subject there. I-I remember a time, we never locked our doors, uh, and I lived in a town, little town of Laurel for a while, and I think even back then, we never locked our doors 'cause nobody, you didn't have to worry about anybody **breaking into** your house or doing anything. And on the farm we never, we'd go away for a weekend and never lock a door. And you didn't worry. As

a kid, I remember at age six or seven, hitchhiking down the road during World War II. We'd go to Fort Meade to use the swimming pool. And we didn't think anything about **hitchhiking**, and you didn't worry about some **dude** picking you up and molesting you or anything like that, just, you just didn't hear about it back then. And then over the years, you just see where they, pretty soon everybody locks their doors, they got three or four locks on their doors, they, their kids can't go out and play in the yard, uh, like they could back in my day, and, uh, the parents just have to watch them every minute.

DEFINITIONS

academic atmosphere: The setting or state that contributes to and fosters academia—education, study, teaching, learning, research, and the exchange of ideas and information.

American Sign Language (ASL): A form of manual communication used by deaf and hard of hearing people in the United States. ASL is an autonomous linguistic system structurally independent from English. It is different from sign languages used in other countries, such as Italian Sign Language or Japanese Sign Language.

Bean Pickers: Manual laborers who harvested beans by hand; in this case, the name of the sports team at the school the speaker attended.

breaking into (break in): To enter illegally, usually by force.

'cause: Short for *because*.

change of the seasons: The transition of the year from spring to summer to fall (autumn) to winter.

cool: A slang expression that means to be desired or desirable, to be with it, to be in vogue, or to be happening.

day job: The primary job by which a person supports himself or herself while attempting to start, pursue, or establish another career. This term is used frequently with reference to musicians, artists, actors, and entertainers, who often work at night.

dude: A slang term for a man or a boy.

Eastern Seaboard: The eastern portion of the United States along the Atlantic Ocean.

flat-bed truck: A truck that has a flat and open back area for carrying cargo.

geek: An awkward person who doesn't fit in. It can also mean a person who possesses a lot of specialized knowledge in a particular field, such as a "computer geek."

geezer: A slang term for an old person.

hitchhiking: Standing or walking along a roadside asking for a ride from people driving by.

interstates: Refers to the major highway system of the United States.

make a buck: To earn money or make a profit.

maths (math): The field of study of numbers and calculation.

musician: Usually *musicians.*

Northeast corridor: The states in the northeastern portion of the United States.

one of the reason: Usually "one of the reasons."

person of color: A person not of the Caucasian race; a nonwhite person.

racially segregated: Separated on the basis of race.

running gag: A joke, funny story, or tale that is told frequently.

segregated society: A society in which the races live largely separated from one another.

slow motion: Moving at less than normal speed.

spotlight: In this context, the center of the focus of attention.

the student: The speaker probably means *students.*

suck on your instrument (usually, **to suck at something**)**:** To not be very good or skilled at playing one's instrument.

underestimate: The speaker probably means *disrespect.*

upbringing: The guided or directed growth of a child by his or her parents or guardian into adulthood.

the West: The western United States.

QUESTIONS AND EXERCISES

1. List what these speakers like about life in the United States.

2. Which speakers have had experiences in the United States similar to yours and why?

3. Which speakers have had experiences most different from yours and why?

4. Describe where you have lived in the United States.

5. What do you like about life in the United States?

6. What is the most difficult thing about living in the United States?

7. Identify three words or phrases in this chapter that are new to you, and write a sentence with each one.

CHAPTER 2

THE FAMILY

In this chapter, interviewees talk about life in their families.

1. A FAMILY IN MARYLAND

MAN: Family. I've been married to my wife for about seventeen, eighteen years. We married young, at the age of twenty-one and twenty-two. And we initially, for years, did not want children. We did a lot of traveling to a number of different countries, and finally, uh, somewhere around thirty-two, thirty-three, I looked at my wife and said, "Well, you're not getting any younger, so if we **wanna** do this, we better go ahead and start working on this." And so we made a decision to have children, and I have a daughter, Caitlin Cherie, who is **four and a half years old, going on fifty**. She's also fluent in **American Sign Language**. In fact, from **day one** in the delivery room, I remember signing to her because I wanted to make this imprint on her brain, this language imprint for visual language, and so, uh, we have a special bond not just because she was my first daughter but also through American Sign Language. Um, it's amazing to me, not coming from a deaf family, to see how language develops in a child who does not use, does not have deafness in the family. But she, uh, uses American Sign Language very, pretty fluently, and we have deaf people in our lives all the time, and so that's been a big help for her. She came, uh, to a program after moving to this area at Gallaudet University called the, um, Child Development Center, and in that program—it's a day care center where they have, uh, parents with deaf children attending the day care center, the teachers are occasionally deaf and it's just a really nice environment. And so she was in that program for about a year and a half. And so that's my daughter Caitlin. I-I love my daughter; I'm so in love with her. Uh, I also have a son who's nine months old; his name is Levi Joseph. And, we are bonding and having fun, and he is at nine months, he's speaking several words, and he has about four-four or five signs. So at this point, living in the area, it's, uh, my wife and two children, a girl and a boy.

INTERVIEWER: Do you have siblings?

MAN: I have, uh, four siblings. I have, uh, an older sister, two younger sisters, and a younger brother. And, uh, they're all in New Jersey, uh, right now. We've recently convinced my mom to move to this area, to the Baltimore, Maryland–D.C. area, so she should be moving down shortly, uh, once her house is sold. But my siblings, uh, remain in New Jersey with the exception of my brother, who I've convinced to go to the University of Maryland, and so he's, uh, just started there in **grad school** at the University of Maryland.

2. ITALIAN ROOTS

Well, the Sardegna side, my m—, I should say, my mother's side and my father's side. Let me start with my father's side, which is also from Sardegna, but my grandfather was a merchant marine traveling the world and had a friend in Detroit and ended his **merchant marine** tour and stayed in Detroit. So, uh, and, uh, but went back to Italy, married someone, brought her back, and then had three boys. My dad's the youngest, and they were born, uh, in the States, and my, one of my uncles fought in World War II, my oldest uncle, you know, uh, he actually fought, I think, partially in Italy, which is kind of interesting, um, and, and then, you know, they mixed in, one of my aunts is Polish and, you know, kind of indicative of the Detroit area, the sort of mix that's there.

My mom's side is a much more complicated side, and my mom is also from Sardegna, but part of her family is from Padova and, uh, Vicenza, the Veneto area, and then one of my great-grandfathers was from Rome, and, uh, was a judge who was sent to Sardegna. So, um, which is kind of interesting, given that there's not a lot of movement, um, in or out of, um, Sardegna. So I have second cousins in Padova, I have, uh, great-uncles in Padova, I have family in Sardegna, family in Vicenza, so it's-it's in that, it's, that's kind of split. And I must have family in Rome, but I don't know, it's just, uh, my mother's never told me, you know, about that.

I have two sisters and one brother. I'm the oldest. Um, and they're all in Michigan. Um, they're also very technical, um. My brother is, has a master's in fluid dynamics—he's an engineer. And, um, one of my sisters was a math major, and, computer science, did artificial intelligence. Uh, another sister was, or is, uh, an engineer. I mean she's not—she's at home with the kids now. So, very, um, technical. Although most of us like to read a lot, which, um, is not always—you don't always see a very technical—and like-liking to read a little bit. So . . .

3. A FAMILY SABBATICAL

I had a great experience when I was a kid. Um, my parents were university professors as well, and when I was a young boy, my father got a **sabbatical leave** and so took the whole family to Europe for a year, uh, during his sabbatical leave, and we traveled all around Western Europe, North Africa, the Middle East, and in the process, we visited, uh, not only the great cities of Europe but lots of the, uh, ancient sites, and so I was, I was exposed to archaeological sites from ancient Rome, Greece, Egypt, uh, throughout the Mediterranean area. And as a little kid, I was just fascinated by all of this and, uh, just, uh, drew up as much ancient history and-and culture as I possibly could at the time and came back fascinated with the study of **antiquities**. And so when I was a kid, I started reading, uh, ancient history and the ancient authors in translation and then later on, took up ancient languages.

4. CHANGING FAMILIES

Gosh, when I first came to the United States: one black-and-white TV about this big, uh. Both my parents worked, so in that sense, I didn't go through a period where my mother didn't work and that kind of 1950s, 1960s sort of thing. I'd have to say that parents are a whole lot busier today than my parents. I mean, when work ended, work ended. And today, with e-mail and, uh, electronic communication, work doesn't really have the kind of boundaries.

5. SIBLINGS

So, I'm one of six. Um, in my family, it-it's three girls and then three boys. And I'm the middle girl. So I have an older sister, and she is a mother of four girls herself, uh, in Minnesota, um, and then I'm here in D.C. And then my younger sister is, uh, back in Minnesota. She is an attorney-editor at West Thompson Publishing, and she has a daughter who will be a year in April. Um, so it's very, it's interesting because my older sister is more a stay-at-home mom. She-she does, like, work in a preschool or whatever, but she doesn't have like a full profession, um, and, but she's like an experienced mom because she's the mother of four daughters, but I actually find myself have more in common with my younger sister, who's just this new mom because she has this other component of working full-time, and so we have a lot more in common in the mothering aspect because of that, I think. Which is, that's interesting to me. Then, um, so Kathy, myself, Lisa, then Tom is the oldest son and he is, he lives in, uh, Minnesota as well. He works for an, he-he's a financial accountant in an agricultural company. Um, sort of the funny fact about him is he's on a **curling** team, which many people don't know about, but he actually plays it and it's very fun to watch, but not a lot of people know about it. Uh, then, my, the middle boy Jim is, he lives in Arlington, Virginia, actually, and he works for, uh, Wells Fargo and he does, sort of, he has this **hybrid** position where he does banking stuff, but he watches the legislative agenda on **the Hill**, and he sort of does the liaison between the banking aspect of that and the legislation. Um, and then the youngest, Patrick, is in Florida, and he is a wine consultant, um, at a Total Wine—it's a company—and he, so people come to him and say, "I'm making whatever for dinner, what kind of wine would you recommend?" And so he does that kind of education, so. He's in Florida now. I forgot 'cause he moved recently. I had him back in Minnesota still 'cause he just graduated from college. I **gotta** remember that he's a **full-fledged** adult now.

6. FAMILY IN NEW ZEALAND

MAN: He was, he was a photographer and had to, uh, travel a lot in his work. And, uh, and, my, I have a sister, and she has a-a large family of-of four children now and, uh, as a matter of fact, every year, I would travel, um, or my family would travel—I have a little family: I-I have a wife and son—we would travel to, uh, to New Zealand just about every year to see them, and, uh, usually it was in the wintertime because summer holidays here is the winter there, you see, it's the opposite way **'round** so we would end up in the kind of bleak season. Um, but, uh, but my sister and I, uh, y-you know, swap each other's, uh, children's interests and, um, my fam—, my mother and father now are very elderly, and they're, my mother is now in her mid-eight—, late-late eighties now so, um, it was very quick, but they are.

INTERVIEWER: Since your-your sister lives, still lives in New Zealand and you live here, what's it like when the two families get together, living in vastly, somewhat vastly different cultures?

MAN: Yes, although it's not vastly different. It's not vastly. There are, um, the interesting thing is that when we come here, the **Kiwis** come here, they expect the Americans to be the same. They expect them to have the same ideas and the same goals and the same attitudes to life, and it's misleadingly not true. So it appears to be more similar than it is. So, somebody coming here would think it was the same, but it isn't. When we get together, um, and we've, I've been fortunate enough, every one of her children has visited here and stayed with me, so I've been able to introduce to them what it's like to live and visit, uh, well, at least in Washington, D.C.

Yes, well, um, the interesting thing about Gallipoli in the First World War was that most people's grandfather fought it, you know what I mean. On my mother's side, all of my-my grandfather's brothers fought at Gallipoli, you know. It was a, it was something that, um, that captured the whole generation that were sent off—and mostly volunteered, by the way—sent off to fight, um, a disastrous invasion, disastrous invasion of Turkey. Winston Churchill's idea, by the way, uh, to do that. And um, the casualties, so—and I recently gave the lecture about Iwo Jima because they're very similar in terms of campaigns—but, um, to give you an example of things that don't usually happen in wars or in battles, for the New Zealanders, for example, the-the casualties nearly equaled the numbers deployed, so that is nearly 100 percent casualty rate, that, which is almost unheard of in battles but, uh, and my grandfather was-was wounded there and he had a lot to say about it. Not to me because the war estranged a lot of families and, uh, and, uh, I didn't really know I had a grandfather until I was twenty. And-and so I was about his age when he went. And then I met him and then ⌈ we talked about it, so ⌉.

INTERVIEWER: ⌊ Why did it estrange families? ⌋

MAN: Because people were changed by it, as they are today in-in wars, all over the world. War changes you. War, uh, alters your understanding, um, with the suffering, the loss, the, uh, the stress. Human relationships alter, people are changed by it, and I'm only speaking in-in a general way. I don't really know—I mean, relationships break up, OK, as well, but there was such a lot of-of people having difficulties, a lot of young people. And there is a picture I have of my grandfather and he's there, a very young man from a young country, and he's dressed in his new uniform and it's 1915 and he's just about to be thrown into the most dreadful, uh, of all experiences and have his friends die and have his, in-in-in terrible circumstances, ⌈ so ⌉.

INTERVIEWER: ⌊Was it the trauma⌋ of that that took a long time for him to discuss it with you?

MAN: Uh, no, no, I don't think so. Um, some people talk about their war experiences and some do not. Um, I think, I think most do not. But that wasn't the reason. It was because, it was a small family reason that he had forged another life and he had another family. And so it wasn't, uh, anyway, he had another life. And so I-I really didn't know much about him until later. I knew my-my relatives on-on my other side, on my mother's side of the family, who-who'd fought at Gallipoli, too, but as I said, it was such a common thing, there were so many, uh, so many sent off to fight in that.

7. MOTHERS AND DAUGHTERS

My mother was one of ten children, so already that meant that she just had a lot more, a lot less attention from her parents and a lot more, um, a lot more people that she had to answer to. Uh, she also came from a very traditional Taiwanese household that all the children did what the father told them to do, and they were very, very well versed in what their duties were, what their responsibilities were, and they-they did those things, they-they did those duties as they were expected. Um, I grew up in this country. I'd say that I'm American before anything, and I-I think that with that comes a certain attitude about how you define your own destiny—you make your own decisions—and this was always a source of friction growing up, on top of the normal friction that you have between say, adolescents and-and parents. I think we had some extra ones that came along, um, from the cultural aspects of it. But I've, the older I get, the more I'm struck by the similarities that we also had. She just had a lot of the same kind of reactions to the world that I've had, and, uh, I didn't recognize them when I was younger. But I think that her, the way that she approaches life—that "Well, you know, whatever happens, happens, and you sort of **just roll with it** and try to make the best of it"— that's sort of how I've approached life, too, and that's- that's colored the way that I've lived my life, and so when I look at some of the, um, stories that she tells of when she was growing up, I think, "Huh, that's the same reaction that I would have had," or, "That's the same thing that I would have done." Um, so, despite the big cultural differences that we had and the-the time differences—you know, she had, she lived fifty years earlier than me—um, there's actually a surprising amount of parallels between us, probably just because I'm her daughter and she's my mother.

8. FATHERS AND DAUGHTERS

WOMAN: Uh, I was born in Evanston, Illinois, which is a suburb of Chicago, and I grew up in the Chicago area, um, all the way through high school. Um, my mother was from the Chicago area, my father was from the South, but when he married my mother, they moved to Chicago and that's where my roots are.

INTERVIEWER: Where in the South was your ⌈father from⌉?

WOMAN: ⌊ My father ⌋ was born in Arkansas, um, in a little town in the northeastern corner of Arkansas called Rector. It's hardly **a dot on the map** but sort of across the river from Memphis, Tennessee.

INTERVIEWER: You ever been there or . . . ?

WOMAN: I have been there, yes. Um, when I was little . . . my father was from a very large family; he was the oldest of nine children, and they all married and had children of their own and on and on and on. And when I was little, um, I think the first time was when I was about six, we went to Arkansas several summers when there was a very large family reunion. Um, my mother had been an only child, and, uh, her mother was an only child, too, so there were very few relatives on my mother's side, and the first time I went to one of these family reunions in Arkansas with all of these people who were related to me, I was astonished. I had no idea that-that I had these many, that many people that were actually related to me. So it was, it was quite an eye-opening experience.

But I must say that, uh, having an actor as a father is a very different sort of family setting from what most children have. I didn't have a father who went to work five days a week, **nine-to-five**, was home all the time on the weekends. Um, when you're an actor, you're a little bit itinerant, and sometimes you may be working a lot, sometimes you may not be working very much. Uh, of course, these actors frequently are working at night, so my father would be home during the day and rather, and working in the evenings. It makes for a very different sort of life experience and growing up experience. But it was also because of that, uh, unpredictability, I guess, um, for me and also for my brother and sister—there were three of us—um, acting was not the sort of lifestyle or career that any of us wanted to pursue. I think all of us

$$\begin{matrix} \text{grew up} \end{matrix} \ldots$$

INTERVIEWER: It kind of turned you off from . . .

WOMAN: Yeah, kind of had the-the idea that it would be much better to have something that had more security attached to it, compared with the glamour, if you will, of being an actor. But it was a wonderful—as a kid growing up—it was a wonderful thing because, um, we met lots of interesting people, acting friends of my father and my mother, um, who were also very down-to-earth people as well but, you know, celebrities and the like, that was kind of fun. But . . .

INTERVIEWER: Did you get to see him perform?

WOMAN: Yes, I did, and that was the most fun thing of all. Um, it's-it's a real unusual experience when one, you have a certain image of your parents, you see them around the house all the time, and then suddenly to see one's father or mother appearing on the **Broadway** stage or in a theater, uh, in costume and saying very different sorts of lines and speeches, uh, is-is really an amazing experience. And I was very, very proud of him for everything that he did.

DEFINITIONS

American Sign Language (ASL): A form of manual communication used by deaf and hard of hearing people in the United States. ASL is an autonomous linguistic system structurally independent from English. It is different from sign languages used in other countries, such as Italian Sign Language or Japanese Sign Language.

antiquities: Ancient civilizations and their remnants, ruins, and history.

Broadway: A major street in New York City, New York, that is synonymous with live theater and is the major theater district of the city.

'cause: Short for *because.*

curling: A team sport similar to bocce and shuffleboard that is played on ice with large granite stones and brooms in which the object is to get your team's "stone" as close as possible to the target while preventing your opponent from doing the same.

day one: The very first day or beginning of an event or period of time.

a dot on the map: A very small town or location.

four and a half years old, going on fifty: An expression that means the speaker's daughter is four and half years old chronologically but exhibits the maturity or mentality of a much older person.

full-fledged: Complete, total, entitled to all the benefits and responsibilities.

gotta: Common verbal utterance of *got to*, which means the same as *have to*.

grad school (graduate school): The collegiate educational level after the first four years of college (baccalaureate) during which a person usually pursues an advanced degree.

the Hill: An expression that refers to the area around the U.S. Capitol Building in Washington, D.C., where the members of Congress (Senate and House of Representatives) and their staffs work. It is the center of the legislative branch of the U.S. federal government.

hybrid: An object or entity that has a mixture or combination of characteristics taken from other things.

just roll with it: An expression that means "to accept a situation or circumstance as it arises and deal with it or adjust to it."

Kiwis: A slang term referring to people from New Zealand, derived from the kiwi bird, which is native to New Zealand.

merchant marine: A nation's publicly or privately owned commercial sailing fleet.

nine-to-five: This term refers to the typical hours that most people work during a five-day workweek, 9:00 A.M. to 5:00 P.M. It is often used to refer to a typical, five-day workweek job.

'round: Short for *around.*

sabbatical leave: At academic institutions, a leave of absence granted to faculty members every seven years, during which they can pursue other interests or activities.

wanna: Want to.

QUESTIONS AND EXERCISES

1. Describe your family. How are the families of these speakers like your family?

2. What kind of work do/did your parents do?

3. How has your family life changed since coming to America?

4. For which speaker do children play a large role? How does that compare to your family or to when you were growing up?

5. What memories do these speakers have of their families?

6. Identify three words or phrases in this chapter that are new to you, and write a sentence with each one.

CHAPTER 3

THE HOME

In this chapter, interviewees talk about their homes.

1. ROW HOUSES

WOMAN: OK, I live in a little **Victorian house**, and, uh, as you walk in, there's a little entrance, and then there's a-a living room and a kitchen—there's an arc and the kitchen is right there, so the kitchen and the living room are together. And then there's a stairway, and upstairs there are two bedrooms and one **full bathroom**, and it also has a little patio.

INTERVIEWER: And what's-what's your favorite room in the house and why?

WOMAN: Um, I think my favori-favorite room is the living room because it's one of these little Victorian houses so it has a-a—one of those windows, um, I don't remember the name of it . . . um, a-a **bay window**—it has a bay window, and, uh, and it's, uh, in, but you can, the stairway, it's very, it's one of those old stairways, so and it's-it's beautiful, and it's right there in the middle of the living room and so you can see the-the stairway and the, it's very light and it's also, we painted the walls yellow, which is a color I like, so and it's comfortable, it's got a nice comfortable couch, and I have my music, uh, stereo there so I can sit and listen to my music.

2. A **LOG HOUSE**

MAN: It's a log house that my **late** wife and I built ourselves, and I also have a three-car log garage that I, that my present wife and I built ourselves. And, uh . . .

INTERVIEWER: How did you decide on that type of house?

MAN: Always wanted a log house. So, bought a kit and built it.

INTERVIEWER: How long did it take you to build it?

MAN: Started in April, uh, and had it **under roof** by August of that year, and then it took from August of that year till the following June to get it **finished out** on the inside, enough to move into it. It was actually, took longer to do the inside than it did to put the logs up. Logs were the easiest part of it. And I had never built anything of that magnitude. I mean, I was a carpenter's helper and, uh, a bricklayer's apprentice and all that business, but I'd never done anything like that. But, uh, the book they give you with the kit pretty much **lays it right out**, and if you had any problems, you called the company and they had an engineer pull out a set of your drawings and you had a set, and you'd tell him what page to go to and he would look at it and say, "What's your problem?" And you'd say, "Well, here's where I'm having a problem." And they would tell you what to do.

Well, when you walk through the front door, the first thing you're going to see is a staircase right in front of you that goes up to the loft, and it's, uh, a **cathedral ceiling**. And off to the right is the living room, which is a sunken living room, it goes down into the, by the fireplace with, um—I want to call it flagstone, like western Maryland stone—big fireplace. And then the kitchen's off from that. And then, the rest of it—you know, bathrooms and bedrooms and that kind of thing. Upstairs is the, in the loft, is where we watch TV and that kind of stuff. And then my radio room is in the back . . . corner.

INTERVIEWER: So what's your favorite room in the house?

MAN: My radio room. That's where I have all my stuff!

INTERVIEWER: Yeah?

MAN: Yeah.

INTERVIEWER: Tell us about why that's your favorite room.

MAN: Well, I can sit in there and work radio—talk to people all over the world on the radio and do different things.

3. WALKING THROUGH THE HOUSE

MAN: OK, now that the renovation is done, it's easier to visualize, but if you walk in my-my front door—we live in a-a town, and the reason I chose the town is because it has a lot, it has lots of trees and it probably reminded me of New Jersey. It's an older town, not too old but, um. Trees. So, there, I have about, a lot of trees on my property. Once you come inside the house, um, into the foyer area, to the left is a living room. Um, beyond the living room is a dining room area. Um, through the dining room, we have a kitchen area that we just finished renovating. We spent about a year and a half without cabinets because we had our cabinets, uh, custom-made and the cabinetmaker assured me that it would only take a few months, so I was zealous and took them off the wall, and it took a lot longer to get them done, and so the kitchen is just, uh, to the right of the dining room. Beyond that, we have a-a back porch with, uh, looking out into a yard area.

The c—, the porch is enclosed, which is nice especially in the spring, uh, summer, and fall. Just off the kitchen, uh, to the left—to the right, rather—we have a family room that has a fireplace. Um, as well, off the kitchen, there's a **mudroom**, where we have a washer and dryer, uh, and a **pantry**, and we have a basement that also, uh, you can enter, uh, from the, or through the kitchen that's, um, recently been refinished and has a new bathroom put down in the basement and a pretty big rec room, recreation room and family area in the basement. Upstairs we have four bedrooms. If you come in the front door just to the right before you go into, uh, the family room, there're stairs that lead to the second floor, and on the second floor, to our right, I guess to the right, is the master **bedroom**—it's just a bedroom with a-a private bathroom, **master bath**—and to the left, we have three bedrooms: my daughter's room, uh, bathroom that used to be my daughter's bathroom, and she's still saying, "It's my bathroom!" but now it's their bathroom, it's the kids' bathroom, uh, and also, we have, uh, my son's bedroom, as well as an office, a pretty large office that my wife and I share.

INTERVIEWER: What's your favorite room in the house and why?

MAN: I would say my favorite room in the house is the living room, and it's probably the, my favorite room because of the co—, the color, for one—it's a very warm color, it's, uh, almost a watermelon-peach type of color, and so it's just very calming when you're in the living room—uh, doesn't receive a lot of traffic, so it's always pristinely organized and-and kept, uh, nice and the piano is also in the living room, and so I have tons of music that, uh, that's hidden in the, not hidden but it's hidden in a cube, an oversize cube, and so all music is inside there, categorized, and I just enjoy, I enjoy the living room, it's-it's an open space, um, very calming and great music comes out of the room.

4. A FAVORITE ROOM

Um, well, as I-I said earlier, I read a lot and I have a very comfortable reading place in my living room, very **comfy** chair right by the window, has good light, and I can play some music if I want to. Um, it's-it's a very comforting place to come home to and enjoy just the-the solitude of a good book or two or three good books.

5. LINCOLN LOGS

WOMAN: But it's **gonna** be a log home, um . . .

MAN: *Cedar* log home.

WOMAN: Cedar.

MAN: Which I apparently have realized in our relationship that I'm the picky one.

WOMAN: Imagine that.

MAN: It's a, it's-it's awesome, it's different from a conventionally stick-built home, which is what they call, you know, what we're in, which is generally [a] . . .

WOMAN: [Framed] . . .

MAN: Framed house, with **two-by-fours**, uh, batting, insulat—, type of insulation, and a kind of dry wall that is either painted or texture coated or something like that.

WOMAN: We are not building it ourselves.

MAN: We are not building it ourselves, which many log homes are built by . . .

WOMAN: The homeowner.

MAN: The homeowner and . . .

WOMAN: Like Bob Simpson.

MAN: Like Bob Simpson. And, um, they're, it's a full, y'know, log, which is shaped as sort of like a *D*, and so you have one round edge on the outside and flat edge, and the inside is the flat edge, and that log is your insulation. Um, they put a very narrow strip on top of the log, and then they stack the logs on top very much like what, the traditional Lincoln log.

Drive up the driveway. We're using the back of our home as the front entrance. Uh, where it is in the woods, we wanted it pictured so that when we're in the house and looking out, we wanted to see the woods and not the driveway. If we had turned it around we'd be seeing the driveway. So we would go in our-our, **quote-unquote**, front door, which is, uh, adjoining our dining room. Uh, we would walk around the dining room; to the right of that would be the kitchen, uh, and the kitchen and dining room both open up into a **great room**. On both sides of the house we have a bedroom on each side and a bathroom on each side—a master bathroom. Um . . .

WOMAN: With a wood-burning stove in the great room.

MAN: Wood-burning stove in the center of the great room, pretty much. And, um, uh . . .

WOMAN: A stairway to go to the loft.

MAN: Uh, a stairway to go to the loft, and, uh, step down to go into a theater room.

INTERVIEWER: Now, so, what-what's your favorite room in the house?

MAN: My favorite room would be, of course, the theater room. It will probably be the most expensive room in the house, as well.

WOMAN: It may be his bedroom . . .

MAN: It may be my bedroom—and it may be my *only* room. But . . . it's, uh, it's a, that's, that will be my favorite room. You know, I feel like I'm sort of taking an ownership to it and getting the, uh, everything laid out in it the way I want to. I want to make it more like a movie theater that's in the house—not, like, a theater *room* that's in, with **surround sound** in—that's in everyone's house. I-I've typically like to, I don't know, maybe, go a little bit too far into the, uh, design phase of that. So, I'm **contracting out** a separate person to do the design, uh, of that room. And he'll also be doing some of the building in there. The walls will have wall treatments in there, there should be maybe either soundboard or some sort of a, um, uh, sound dampener on the walls. Uh, there will be curtains. Most, uh, family rooms that have theater, theater room atmosphere don't have curtains. This should have that. Um, just to give the idea.

WOMAN: There's no windows in that part of the house.

MAN: There'll be no windows in that part of the house. There's only one door, uh . . .

WOMAN: They got to pay admission to get in.

MAN: Right!

WOMAN: I think that's what he . . .

INTERVIEWER: So that, what's it for?

MAN: It-it's to view movies. I-I will also use it—it will have the capability to probably have television, ah, pictured on an over hundred-inch screen. Uh, but, primarily for movies. It will be used as a theater the way a theater is conventionally used. So when you come in, there'll be a quiet swinging door that will open, close behind you. If you come in the middle of a picture, you don't want to talk, you want to be quiet and courteous to other people watching the film. Um, that's sort of . . .

WOMAN: There may be a trapdoor to let them out, down the bottom.

MAN: There will not be any of that.

WOMAN: If they're too loud.

INTERVIEWER: What's your favorite room?

WOMAN: It's probably going to be the kitchen, because I do like to cook. Um, so, I think it's going to be the kitchen.

MAN: Ah, it's definitely the kitchen.

WOMAN: It-it'll have to be the kitchen. I like to eat, too, so.

MAN: I'm going to like the kitchen, too.

WOMAN: Oh, no, you're not.

6. LIVING AT THE **DROP ZONE**

WOMAN: Our house is a little unusual because we live at an airport, so, uh, you know, we have a, sort of like an apartment attached to the hangar, um. So actually if you came in the front, you would be in, uh, what would be the ⎡restroom for the-the hangar⎤.

MAN: ⎣   Well, this is actually the   ⎦ front door here.

WOMAN: Yeah, OK, well, go ahead.

MAN: It's a sliding glass door—you come in that door and you're in our living room. That restroom is actually for the people that use the skydiving school in the airport, and we normally keep that door closed and don't come through there except in the wintertime when people's not here and the snow's piled up too deep out there to get in that door. Then to the right of this thousand-square-foot room, there's a small office where I'm trying to start to do most of my work from—I'm trying to get out of my office in town. I wanna sell that building and **dispose of** that. And then, uh, we have a huge bedroom to my left and a nice bathroom back there for ourselves, so it's-it's only about thirteen hundred square feet. It's very small—it's very modest in American standards—but if you go to any European nation and you have a twelve-hundred-square-foot house, you're doing **pretty good**.

WOMAN: On thirty-three acres.

MAN: Yeah, on thirty-three acres of land with your own runway and your four-thousand-square-foot garage with your airplane, your motor home, your two motor-cycles, your Corvette, your pickup truck, et cetera, et cetera. Which is very unusual. Most people have a four-thousand-square-foot house and a twelve-hundred-square-foot garage. We have it the other way around 'cause we're never inside living. We're always outside living.

DEFINITIONS

bay window: A kind of window that, instead of being flush with the exterior wall of the house, extends outward, usually with a windowsill large enough to hold objects such as potted plants or for a person to sit.

cathedral ceiling: A high vaulted ceiling similar to that found in a church or cathedral.

comfy: Slang for or shortening of the word *comfortable*.

contracting out: Hiring a contractor to do work.

disclose of: The speaker probably intends to say "dispose of," which means "to sell [in this case], get rid of, throw away, or relinquish ownership of."

drop zone: An area or business devoted to skydiving.

finished out: Completed construction.

full bathroom: In American houses, a bathroom that has a sink, toilet, and shower or tub.

gonna: Going to.

great room: A large living room.

late: Deceased, dead.

lays it right out: To explain something or give a clear illustration or presentation of it.

Lincoln logs: A children's toy consisting of a set of wooden or plastic logs of varying sizes, from which a child could construct various kinds of houses or other structures by interlocking the logs together. The toy is named after Abraham Lincoln, a former President of the United States, who lived in a log home as a child.

log house: A house made of logs. This kind of house had its origin in the time of the original settlement of the United States. The logs were trees that had been cut down, shaped, and fixed together.

master bedroom, master bath: The largest, or main, bedroom or bathroom in a house.

mudroom: A small room where people can remove their dirty or muddy footwear before entering the rest of the house.

pantry: A relatively small closet-type storage room.

pretty good: Very good.

quote-unquote: A phrase that is used to indicate the statement following it is a direct quotation.

row houses: Houses built side by side and attached to the ones next to them.

surround sound: A feature of a stereo or sound system that makes the sound appear to be coming from all directions around the listener.

two-by-fours: Pieces of wood used in construction that are roughly two inches thick and four inches wide of varying lengths.

under roof: Completed to the point that the roof has been put in place.

Victorian house: A style of house similar to those popular during the Victorian era of England.

QUESTIONS AND EXERCISES

1. Which of these speakers has the most unusual home and why?

2. Whose home is most similar to yours and why?

3. Describe the house that you grew up in.

4. Which is your favorite room in the house where you live now and why?

5. How do homes in the United States differ from homes where you grew up and why?

6. Identify three words or phrases in this chapter that are new to you, and write a sentence with each one.

The Home

CHAPTER 4

THE ROLE OF WOMEN

In this chapter, interviewees talk about the sometimes-changing role of women in the United States and in their countries of origin.

1. A GOOD WIFE

My mother, my mother wanted me to be a doctor. I don't have the temp—, really, the temperament for it. She wanted me to be a doctor, but at the same time, a really good wife. And I think my-my mom was kind of just torn in those, you know, in the two ways, and it was this idea that you had—mother, wife—that was, you know, number one. And she just says, y'know, she wishes things were different when she were, when she was younger 'cause it was a bit harder. My nieces, um, I think my sister didn't have to worry 'cause I think my, the one niece has a **pretty good head**-head **on her shoulders** and thought it, you know, was an easy class, something that was kind of interesting, you know, like that, but she's pretty focused, and I think-think she won't have that guilt that, you know, my mom certainly had and, you know, I had a little bit of that, you know, being Catholic. That's something you deal with, I think, and also with women, I think there's this, um, so, but I think it's good because there were contemporaries of mine whose, like, their parents didn't want them to be doctors, they wanted them to be nurses, you know. My mom, at least, my par—, and my dad, too, you know, "Well, be a doctor—just be a good wife," so.

2. OPTIONS

I think that I'm a more, um, I'm more cognizant of my role as a mother. So I-I purposely think about that role and-and our relationship where I think my mom, because of circumstances, it, she was a mother and she was just doing mothering things. I don't think she thought of it more as something that you could, I don't know, plan for or-or perfect in any way. I'm not saying I'm good at it, but I just have thought about it so I did research about thi—, certain things ahead of time, to sort of anticipate things, um, and because of that, I-I don't think I felt as overwhelmed by the, by that role, so I've enjoyed it more, and I think that our relationship has—you know, in the twenty-three months that it's been around—has, i-it's-it's more, it's not as stressed, I don't feel like, I don't feel like, I mean, at twenty-three months, I can't remember what my relationship was like with my mother, but, um, I do remember as I was older that, you know, it was some-thing that she had to do and, she had, you know, she had to clean the house and we had to get things done and let's move, and there was less, "OK, so what's going on? Tell me what's, what are you, what did you do today?" or whatever, um, where I thi—, I-I have that more with Aida. Um, also my mother had six children, so that reduces the time you can sp—, allocate to one individual, where I don't have that re—, constraint.

I remember, um, my mom went to college, and I remember her telling me that she had the option of either becoming a nurse or becoming a teacher. Um, I never felt that I had those two options. Um, so I think choice is one big difference, um. I-I-I guess there were three roles. I guess you could become a nurse, become a teacher until you became a mother. I think that's sort of how she had it all **laid out**, um, where I never, I never felt that there was just those three options—I think that-that's a big difference.

So I think that's one-one big one is just what are your options for the future, what-what do you want to be. Um, I f—, I feel like that sort of trickles down into all areas of your life. I think if you-you have, if it's very clear you have these three options, then everything gets narrowed down and so you exclude other things because, I mean, what would be the point of pursuing anything else if tho—, if that's where you're headed? Um, I think one significant difference is my access to sports. Um, that is a-a defin-ing, like, characteristic of my background, growing up, and I was always involved in sports, and it really opened doors, like it brought me to a college I never would have dreamed of going to because I didn't even know about it, but they recruited me, so then I went and I was like, "Oh, love this place. Let's go here." Uh, where my mom, although I know she's a tremendously athletic woman, she, they didn't have sports teams when she was in school, um. And, so I think that is a huge-huge difference, the impact of having that opportunity was just tremendous. Um, and I was, I think I'm a product of that sort of first generation that had, like, access to sports teams from the very beginning. So when I started, like, when I was really young—in kindergarten—it was gymnastics, and that was still the most common sports outlet for young girls. But quickly, the soccer sort of—you know, basketball, volleyball—that started to sort of **trickle down** and they started introducing it like in fourth and fifth grade, that happened right as I was getting to fourth and fifth grade, and so I got, "Oh, well, I like gymnastics a lot, but I like volleyball a lot more," you know, so, I-I mean, that's, I think has made one of the biggest impacts on my life, in the course of my life.

3. WORKING MOMS

WOMAN: We could actually compare his mother to my mother.

MAN: Right, that's better.

WOMAN: Which is a really good comparison . . .

INTERVIEWER: OK, OK.

WOMAN: Because my mom was a single mom and had to raise three of us on her own limited income, um, and his mom was not, so your mom, ⎡ so your mom ⎤ . . .

MAN: ⎣My mom, my-⎦ my mom was fortunate enough that she could take time off of work when she had our, us—me and my brother—and raised us primarily while my-my father had started his own business and kept that going to help support the family. That was the way I think most families did it in that, in that time period. We, um . . .

WOMAN: And then when your mom went back to work, ⌈she only⌉ worked part-time.

MAN: ⌊She only,⌋ she only went back part-time, and she did that to just have the extra **spending money** and, uh . . .

WOMAN: And to feel like she had her own life and independence.

MAN: Right, right, but she didn't feel comfortable managing that **full-time**. Um, nowadays, I really feel like there's a two-income house. You need two incomes to support any household with children. That's sort of the way I feel it is. Uh, I've often said that if I were ever to have children, that I would, uh, I would, at the very, very basic end of it, would not do anything less than provide them what my parents provided me.

4. CHANGING PERSPECTIVES

Boy, that's an interesting subject. Um, well, I think there was a point in time where somebody said that staying home and taking care of your kids was demeaning to a woman, and a lot of them bought into that, and now I think it's sort of going the other way. Some women are saying, "Well, I've been the-the route of, you know, being a corporate lawyer," or whatever, and now they say more women are having ailments that were attributed to men more because they were out in the workforce and they were the high-powered executives. Now the women are, and they're-they're having to put up with these stresses that the men were putting up with. So now they say, "Well, you know, maybe staying home and taking care

of the kids wasn't so bad." So they're, you know, some of
'em are changing, some of 'em aren't. But, uh, who knows
who's **gonna** sort that out?

5. BALANCING WORK AND FAMILY

I-I don't know that I balance it that well. I think I kind
of **swing back and forth**, um, pouring too much of my
energy maybe i-in, more of my energy than is reason-
able into my job for a period of time, and then swinging
back and being very, very, uh, insistent on spending extra
time with my family. So maybe in, I like to think that
in the long run, it balances out, but it's true that there
are moments when you realize that you've spent all your
time on work things and you have hardly seen your family. Um, I-I think that's probably symptomatic of the way
that it is for working mothers in the country in general.
I-I've-I've, you know, everyone's heard the stories of how
it's so much better in more progressive countries, the
countries that have more progressive laws for working
mothers. It's just, um, it-it's-it's challenging here. I-I think
that everyone tries to do their best at it, and my way isn't

the same way as everybody's else's but, um, there's always room for improvement, so it's one of the areas that I'm-I'm still working on, balancing a little bit more equitably.

6. CULTURAL DIFFERENCES

MAN: As I said, I think women work much harder here, and, of course, they have, uh, more rights here. They have freedom of speech. I mean, they-they have more independence here, they have more money here, uh, but, uh, they work too-too much here. I mean, uh, as I said, doing from laundry, housework, house chores, I mean, they are too much. I mean, by the t—, I-I have seen my wife virtually doing nothing in India to doing everything here, so. Women, I mean, of course, she is much more independent, she doesn't have to ask me ever because she does her own job, she has her own money. She can just walk in and buy anything and **trash it** next day. I mean, nobody is going to ask a question why she did that. Lot of independence, I mean, uh, and they see, the women around here have lot of, uh, independence themselves, there's no cultural ba—, uh, barriers, there's no, I mean, the best thing about America is that you've all kind of people from all over the world, they live here together, harmoniously. And, uh, the women back home in India, they are like, uh, men are the head of the family, so if-if my child is born, the certificate will carry my-my name—my son's name—so birth certificate will have my name. But same thing, if it is here, the mother's name will be there, so it's-it's a two different worlds altogether. Women, I think, uh, they work much harder, but I think Indian women here, they're happier because they get something they can never think of in India—independence, yeah.

My mother could never say, uh, anything to my father. Uh, my mother had to pray to God that he says, "Let's go for a movie." And, uh, she could not say that, "Oh, we want to go for a movie." He has to—she had to suggest in a different way, "Oh," that, "I was talking to that neighbor and, uh, she went for a movie," so the father has to catch, and if he's not in a good mood, he will say, "OK, OK, that's fine." So she had to pray for him to suggest something so we can, we can get it because he's the man who decides because he has money. But my wife, I mean, she's much independent here, and if I say I'm tired, she picks her own car and go. So it's-it's like two extremes. But, uh, I think—**by and large** I-I-I feel—there-there is a generation gap, too, of course, and, uh, my wife would not have been like my mother back home if we were in India. She would have been little more independent, but, of course, she is much more independent here because she drives herself, she has her own money, she has, uh, I mean, uh, she has a good job, so there's a lot of differences.

INTERVIEWER: A lot of differences.

DEFINITIONS

by and large: An expression that means "generally speaking," "for the most part," or " in most cases."

'em: Common shortened pronunciation of *them*.

full-time: Working at a job or a task for all of the time specified or needed to accomplish it. When used in reference to work, it usually means working at a job for forty hours per week.

gonna: Going to.

laid out: Predetermined.

pretty good head on her shoulders: An expression that means "to have good judgment or be a sound or circumspect thinker."

spending money: Money that can be used for any desired purpose, usually for pleasure, in contrast to money that has to be used for a specific purpose.

swing back and forth: To move or alternate between two different positions or points of view.

trash it: To discard, throw away, or vandalize something.

trickle down: The flow of something from one level or area to another.

QUESTIONS AND EXERCISES

1. What kinds of changes in women's roles do these speakers describe?

2. How is the role of women in the United States different from the role of women in other countries?

3. How is the life of your sister or wife different from that of your mother?

4. What do you think explains the changing role of women?

5. How do you expect women's roles to change in the future?

6. Identify three words or phrases in this chapter that are new to you, and write a sentence with each one.

CHAPTER 5

EDUCATION

In this chapter, interviewees describe their educational experiences.

1. SCHOOL IN PHILADELPHIA

I had a, I grew up in Philadelphia, uh. So, in **Philly**, I started in local schools, um, I guess **nursing school** they started with, **Pre-K**, and, uh—not sure how detailed you want, but if it's a year-by-year thing—uh, my, the thing in-in Philly, the, in a, in grade school, the, in Philadelphia in particular—and I don't know if other cities do it—but it had a fabulous system where it was, there's kind of two systems on top of each other where there's a local school, uh, and then there's also what they in Philly called **magnet schools** that pulled kids, uh, from all around to a different program, uh. So in, up until like fourth grade or something, I had a school where I went to four days a week, and then there was a different one that I went to that, I think that kept changing the name—it was ac—, you know, academically talented or gifted—they changed the name a number of times, but there was a different building, a different school you would go to the fifth day a week, um. And it was, as a kid, one of the big things is that you don't, you know, I took—well, they didn't have school buses—so you took, I took city buses to school starting in probably **third grade**, uh, and, I guess I had an older brother who would go with me, but, uh, somewhere in there he went off to a different school, and I'm taking the bus to school at, you know, age, you know, nine or eight or something, which I don't think they let kids do anymore. Uh, but you would, uh, that school—I always left each school one year before it was capped out. My elementary school went to **fifth**. I left after fourth grade and went to a different school that did fifth through eighth, uh, and then that school went actually through twelfth, but I left after eighth grade, after, uh, junior high, and that was a, uh, that school was called, uh, Masterman—it was somebody's name: Julia Masterman, uh, Middle School. And that school was, that was a magnet school, so from my elementary school, I had to apply to get into that school, uh, and you had to have certain grades to get in, I mean, as a **fifth grader**, um, and that—I think, I'm not sure, but I think my dad had to go into the office and-and push a little bit to get me in, uh, but he did—and that school was downtown, uh, so again I'm taking the bus and the subway to school every day, uh, from age ten, um. And I went there through junior high and then went to, uh, again a magnet school, so it wasn't my local high school, um, uh, High School of Engineering and Science, um, which was a couple blocks, about three or four blocks off campus from Temple University. And there they had a program where you did, uh, tenth, you did, uh, two years of English in eleventh grade, and English was the only class you needed four years of, which is why you did both years of it in the one year, and then, uh, and this was for the top sixty-some kids out of maybe a hundred and fifty, uh, they took those kids, gave them two years of English, and then you were done your high school ed—, you know, requirements, uh, and they waived a year of **gym**, I think, of **phys ed** and sent you to Temple University for a year instead of twelfth grade. Uh, so that's what I did.

2. GETTING RECRUITED

WOMAN: Um, I **ran track**—well, I-I played volleyball, basketball, and track in high school, but, um, I was recruited to run track for the Brown University track team. And um, like I said, I didn't, I was, little **hick town**, you know, farm girl. **Ivy League**, East Coast, what is all that? I didn't know. And I had gotten this information from this university, and I was reading it, and reading about the university in general, not only the track team but the university in general, and I said, "**Gosh**, this has, like, all the characteristics that I would dream up in an ideal school." And they have a track team and, that seems somewhat interested, and so I said, "Well, I'll check it out." And so they **flew me out there** and Providence, Rhode Island, you know, it was beautiful, loved the campus, loved the team. So, it, if it hadn't, I just, if it hadn't been for track and doing well in track, I, why would they care, you know, about this little girl in Middle of Nowhere, Minnesota?

INTERVIEWER: But it **opened a lot of doors** and gave you opportunities?

WOMAN: Exactly, because then it, there I was at this, you know, Ivy League school, and, you know, just trem—, I was a history **major** and focused on American history, and, you know, I have as my advisor, Gordon Wood, the authority on the American Revolutionary War, you know. It was amazing. It was like, you don't get that. I couldn't have dreamt that. And then you're around these brilliant people—I don't know who I fooled to get in there—but, you know, your friends are just amazing and everyone has, comes from these just fascinating backgrounds . . .

3. A **LIBERAL ARTS EDUCATION**

Well, at the-the, at the university level, one difference is that, um, in Spain, we don't have the concept of a liberal arts education. So, uh, when you, by the time you're eighteen and you decide to go to college, you have to know what you wanna do, so you want to be a doctor or a lawyer, whatever, you have to know. And you go straight into that field. And it's actually, for some fields, it's actually quite competitive, so, uh, for example, if you want to go into **med school**, you better have like a **Plan B** and a **Plan C**, so you say, "OK, med school is my first choice, but then, uh, biology is my second choice, and pharmacy is my third choice," for example. And then depending on what grade you get on your **access exam**, then-then you can get into one field or another, and then there are other fields that are not so competitive. Um, but-but yeah, but the difference is that you have to know what you want to do by the time you go to college, whereas here, you know, the concept of a liberal arts education is completely different. Basically, you go to college to learn about, uh, a lot of things, to get a general education about a bunch of fields, and then, uh, after that you decide what you want to **major in**.

4. THE SCHOOL NEWSPAPER

STUDENT: I'm-I'm on the newspaper, and, uh, I just recently got on—and pretty early for a **sophomore**, so. We'll see how it pans out. If I like it a lot then that might be something I'm interested in pursuing.

INTERVIEWER: How often does the newspaper **come out**?

STUDENT: Uh, I believe the newspaper comes out once a month, which is not that often, but for a school paper, it's better than most, and it's-it's a really big paper so there's a lot going into it.

INTERVIEWER: Describe the process of getting it ready every month. What has to happen?

STUDENT: Well, first, um, we have a meeting, uh, trying to find article ideas, and basically everyone who knows someone interesting or something newsworthy, we just write it on the board, and then our sponsor, Mr. Keegan, he hands out the, uh, the articles. So we then have to go interview people, and, um, you have to have a recorder and have your questions all ready and then we write it, using a quote, I mean a lot of quotes. And then, um, then we submit it, um, to the, to the drive on the computers, and then the editors look over it. And then they paste it up on boards, on how the comp—, the, uh, newspaper layout would be and—it's called **pasteup**—and, uh, then everyone edits your articles so you can't be very **touchy** about that kind of thing, um. And you edit other people's articles, and then, um, the pasteups, uh, get fixed, and so we put on new ones and then they're sent to the printers. And we print in color, so it's kind of costly.

5. AN INDIAN PERSPECTIVE

MAN: I'm trying to cope with American, uh, education system because my son goes to school, and I'm-I'm very interested to see what kind of education is he getting because I want him—naturally, as I said, I want him to go to Harvard University eventually, to the best college in-in the country. So I want him to be, so I-I look at his homework, I see the kind of, uh, I ask him, "What kind of interaction, uh, you have?" And, uh, also, so I see, uh, in, he's in grade three and he has to do lot of book reports. He has to do science projects, grade three. Of course, it's Howard County, so the educational level is a little high, but I have, I have to work hard, I have to take out at least an hour or two a day to understand the kind of project he has. My wife does all the **book reports** with him because it's English—her English is better than mine, and, uh, so. And I do all the science projects, all-all-all that projects so I have study myself and understand and then make him understand. I-I don't think that I ever did so, but I called my brother whose son is also in the, daughter is in the same age and, uh, he tells me that they don't have all that. Either he's not paying attention, or, uh, they don't have that, so I think American, uh, education system emph—, there's a lot of emphasis on if they try to make you a good salesperson. I think it's all about marketing, about sales so they, whatever they-they, I mean, he has to do lot of presentations in school, so all that public speaking, uh, it's easy for him. And, uh, of course, yeah, there's lot of emphasis on the vocabulary, there's a lot of emphasis on the spellings, which we never had. I still have **bad spellings**, so.

But, I'm very happy with America's education system, but what I hear from my sister-in-law is, when they go into the high school, then I have to be little more vigilant. You can't say anything, but you just have to lead him by the example. So far, touch with my son is pretty good. He's a very good human being, I mean, uh, he really is—there's a lot of respect for-for people, I hope he continues to be with the same American education system.

INTERVIEWER: Did you, was your system basically a British system, with forms and . . . ?

MAN: Yes, a lot of, we are basically, all-all Indian systems are British systems. We never had any system unless they came and made some, so, uh. Most, it's like there're a lot of forms, as you said. There're a lot, ev—, for everything, you have to get permission, uh, so, it's-it's pretty good. There's a lot of, emphasis in India is on memory, that you have to memorize a lot of stuff so, which is good. I mean, in my time, I never had to use calculator. I started using calculator when I went into job and I never had to use calculator. I always did calculation with my hand and break it down and make it easy. But, uh, my son was asking me how he needs a calculator, so I just said, "No," even though the teacher said it's OK. So I-I-I, there some good things in India, but I think mostly the overall education system here is good. I hope it continues to be like that when he goes to middle school or high school.

DEFINITIONS

access exam: An entrance exam that is required for entry into a particular school or field of study.

bad spellings (usually **bad spelling** or **poor spelling**): The inability to spell words correctly.

book reports: Reviews of books that a student has been required to read.

come out: In this context, published.

fifth: Fifth grade in an elementary education.

fifth grader: A child in the fifth grade.

flew me out there: A phrase that means "to arrange for one's transportation by plane."

gosh: An exclamation.

gym: Short for *gymnasium*; also used to refer to physical education class in schools.

hick town: A rural, unsophisticated, or backward town.

Ivy League: An athletic conference in the northeastern United States comprising eight universities: Brown, Columbia, Cornell, Dartmouth, Harvard, Penn, Princeton, and Yale. The term is also synonymous with academic excellence and prestige.

liberal arts education: A college education offered by some institutions in the United States, in which undergraduates are required to take a wide range of courses in addition to specializing in one specific area of study, before they are awarded a degree.

magnet schools: A kind of secondary school that offers a specialized curriculum or courses.

major: The field or subject that a student has chosen as his or her primary area of study.

major in: To pursue a specific field of study.

med school: Short for *medical school.* An educational institution where students study medicine in order to become doctors.

nursing school: The speaker probably means "nursery school," a school for children under five years of age.

opened a lot of doors: Provided or created opportunities.

pasteup: In printing or journalism, the process of preparing a sample of how the finished printed page will look. This was originally done by actually pasting samples of articles or pictures onto a sheet of paper or cardboard. This process has largely been superseded by computerized page design.

Philly: Common nickname for the city of Philadelphia.

phys ed: Short for *physical education.* A class in school devoted to physical activity such as sports and physical fitness.

Plan B, Plan C: Expressions that mean "a backup plan (B for secondary; C for tertiary) or method for doing something."

Pre-K: School for children before kindergarten.

ran track: To have participated in running events of track and field.

sophomore: In American secondary education, the tenth grade. At the college or university level, it indicates the second year.

third grade: The third of twelve levels in standard American primary education.

touchy: Being sensitive to something.

QUESTIONS AND EXERCISES

1. What are the similarities and differences between your educational experience and that of these speakers?

2. What differences do these speakers see between education in the United States and education in other countries?

3. Describe your own educational experience in detail.

4. Describe the educational experience of a friend or classmate and explain how it is different from your own.

5. Pick one of these speakers and summarize what he or she says was the most challenging part of his or her educational experience.

6. Identify three words or phrases in this chapter that are new to you, and write a sentence with each one.

CHAPTER 6

RECREATION AND ENTERTAINMENT

In this chapter, interviewees talk about what they do in their free time.

1. RVs AND HORSES

MAN: Skydive, **scuba dive**, **hang glide**, **BASE jump**, fly, **hang out** with friends, drink beer, go out to see bands—the list goes on. Always looking for something new and adventurous to do. Some new place to explore. Love to travel the world, see different cultures, interact with people. Stay away from the **touristy** places and go to the things off the beaten path to see how people in other areas of the world really live and interact with each other and experience, uh, places as a local instead of as a tourist.

WOMAN: We have an **RV**. We like to travel around in that, and we avoid the cities, usually. We stick to the country and like he said, the **off the beaten path** places.

INTERVIEWER: Uh-hmm. So what's the last trip you took—I mean, and what was that? Where'd you go?

WOMAN: We went, uh, down through Virginia. We went to Mount Vernon, uh, George Washington's home and um, and then down through . . .

MAN: Jamestown, Yorktown, the beginning of this nation—well, so they say, but really the Spaniards were in St. Augustine before the English were in Jamestown—but it was very interesting to learn all about that stuff.

WOMAN: Uh, I've been **riding** since I was about seven or eight years old, and, uh, I enjoy it as a sport. I compete, but I think I also just like the relationship with the animal.

MAN: We joke that it's her second boyfriend.

WOMAN: Yeah, we call him my second boyfriend. But uh, yeah, I like to train for stuff, uh, you know, and try and get better at it, and, uh, it's a fun sport because it's always changing, you know, and he's really like a partner and you-you can't tell what he's **gonna** do next, so it-it keeps it interesting. Every day is different when I go out there, but I just like to be around him. It's . . .

INTERVIEWER: In what events do you compete?

WOMAN: I do eventing, uh, which has, uh, three phases to it: there's **dressage**, which is **flat work**—it's kind of like ballet on horseback. And, uh, then there's cross-country jumping, where you jump natural obstacles over about a mile-long course and, uh, it's timed for speed and, uh. And then stadium jumping, which is jumping inside a ring, and then you're-you're graded on all three of those, and then there's one grand winner out of all of that, so

it's fun .

INTERVIEWER: What was the last competition like?

WOMAN: Uh, actually, I got eliminated. My horse is still young, and, uh, there was a jump that had one big white mum underneath it and, you know. They-they're animals that are trying to survive, you know, they still have, uh, instincts to survive, and I guess he thought that mum was gonna eat him. So he, uh, stopped three times, which wipes you out of the competition when you have refusals, so, yeah. But we'll keep trying.

INTERVIEWER: So tell me about the horse.

WOMAN: The horse is, uh, I've had him for three years. He's a Connemara Thoroughbred. Connemaras are from Ireland and, um, you know, Thoroughbred. And, uh, he's just spooky and **full of himself** and likes to make life more interesting than what it is, so . . .

2. COMPUTER GAMES

STUDENT: Um, not so much **computer games** as mostly video games. Um, but on the computer I'll just go to a game website, and usually they have new games which I can play on there.

INTERVIEWER: What kind of video games do you play?

STUDENT: Um, mostly fighting games where you just beat up a lot of people, but sometimes I'll play a game that actually has a plot. Um, when they have a plot, I like it to be a long game instead of just a mediocre or short plot that doesn't take that long to finish.

INTERVIEWER: For, like what, for example? Tell me about one in particular.

STUDENT: Well, this one game I like, *Paper Mario*, somehow this guy finds enchanted crystals, and he has to use their power to destroy an evil that took over the world a thousand years ago, got locked by these special crystals, but it's coming back because the crystals have been found by someone evil. And I've gotten to the final boss of the game and I still can't beat it. I, so, I go and I train and train and I come back and I still lose. I need to work on that.

3. STOPPER AND SWEEPER

STUDENT: I play soccer. I'm, um, a defense player. Uh, I play **stopper** and **sweeper**.

INTERVIEWER: Stopper and sweeper?

STUDENT: Yeah, in the lineup. It's like, uh, stopper is in front of the person in front of the **goalie** and sweeper is in front of the goalie.

INTERVIEWER: OK. Are you good?

STUDENT: Uh, I've been playing since fourth grade, so I would hope so. Um, I used to play for my middle school for two years but, um, it was, it consumed a lot of my time, so when I got to high school, I didn't want to do that, and then all I found out that all the soccer players at high school were kind of like slaves to the coaches and they didn't have a lot of free time.

INTERVIEWER: So do you play as part of a school activity or as part of a league outside of school?

STUDENT: I play for, uh, **MSI**, which is a league outside of the school. I still play, yeah.

4. RUNNING

INTERVIEWER: What do you do in your free time? ⌈ If you have free time . . . ⌉

MAN: ⌊Free time, well, uh, yeah—⌋ I love to travel. I go, uh, go back to Europe not just for research and excavation at, uh, at Pompeii, but I love travel and so, uh, get around Italy as much as possible and other places in Western Europe. But I'm also an **outdoorsman**. I enjoy athletic activity. I run a lot, uh, I bicycle quite a bit, um, I swim when I can, uh, I used to be a skydiver, which was, uh, a lot of fun. I don't that much anymore but, uh, but I enjoy being out of doors.

Um, I've always enjoyed running since I was a kid, uh, especially long distances. It's, uh, it's a challenge but it's also a kind of physical activity I just, I very much enjoy. I love being able to run for an hour or two, uh, or three or four at a time. It's, uh, it's something that, uh, that I enjoy. Just the feeling of being in good condition, of course, and having a strong body is-is satisfactory. But more than that, uh, being able to run for extended periods of time, uh, gives me time to think—it, uh, it's a relaxing kind of time for me, gives me plenty of time to reflect or think about, uh, work or, uh, outside creative projects that I have under way, gives plenty of time for ideas to-to ferment. But also, too, uh, frequently I run with an **iPod** and I have digital books, uh, digital recordings of books on my iPod and so I'm able to listen to books as I run, and so, if you're running for a couple of hours at a time, you can get through a fair amount of a book that way. And-and this way, I-I'm able to listen to books that, uh, I might not ordinarily have time to read outside of work.

Consistent running on a regular basis, uh, for a long period of time is the best-best training for a marathon. Um, it's, running twenty-six miles and doing so without dying is not something you can, you can just do on a whim, especially at my age. And so, um, good preparation for a marathon is running, uh, at least thirty-five miles a week for at least ten or twelve weeks, uh, prior to the marathon. So I usually, uh, I usually have training runs, uh, do two or three training runs of somewhere between, uh, seven and ten miles a week, and then on the weekend, I do a long run of at least fifteen. And, uh, so, if I am interested, if I have a target time and I wish to improve my time in a marathon, I will increase my training runs from, uh, from maybe to-to eight to twelve miles each and from three on average a week, to four, say, and then increase the length of my long runs on the weekend as well. But, uh, now that I'm, I've become a certain age, I also benefit from cross-training: riding a stationary bike, uh, swimming a lot, uh, doing, undertaking other, uh, exercises, um, that, um, keep the rest of my body vigorous, not just my legs but are also, uh, less of an impact on my body or less stressful for an-an aging body.

5. CLIMBING MOUNTAINS

INTERVIEWER: So I know that you have a lot of outdoor activities. So talk about that.

WOMAN: Well, about five or six years ago, uh, I had a job where I had money so I could actually afford to buy camping equipment, and I became a member of REI, the outdoor cloth—, the outdoor store. It's Recreational Equipment Incorporated, REI. So I started buying equipment from there and in my home in Oregon—I lived there for the past eleven years—and we have a famous mountain there called Mount Hood. And so my friends and I—hearing friends who can **sign**—I joined them and we went, uh, climbing. We would start at midnight and climb up the mountain in the snow overnight, and then the snow would freeze and so you can use your clamps on the backs, bottom of your shoes, and hike up the mountain, and you'd think it's not that bad—it's only a mile or so—but it took me eight hours to get all the way to the top because it was so hard to breathe. But it was a great experience, and once we got to the top, I can't explain the feeling. It was just a wonderful experience, a great feeling and, just to stand at the top of the mountain and-and look out down below. But the wind was-was terrible up there. And then, after I looked around for a while, I had to get back down the mountain, and to get back down the mountain, I used an ice axe, a pick axe, and had to push, put that into the side of the mountain to be able to slide down and . . . The next day, I had bruises all over me from sliding down the mountain, but it was a really great experience.

6. THE SOCCER LEAGUE

MAN: If I can come across some free time, which, uh, I, uh, well, I-I like making time for myself and my family. Um, I like spending time with my kids, uh, and my wife, uh, but also, if I'm not doing that, I try to, I play a lot of soccer during the weekends and tennis during the weekdays.

INTERVIEWER: Do you play in a-a soccer league?

MAN: Yes, um, I, um, I used to play, uh, when I was back home, at a very high level, um, so when I came here, I came on a soccer scholarship so I was, uh, **All-American** for four years, playing soccer in Oklahoma. And, uh, when I graduated, the intention was to play in the professional league, the **MLS**, uh, but the way the story goes, usually if you do not have your green card at the time when you're supposed to play, uh, you're considered not eligible to work, and as such, you cannot play on the team unless you adjust your status. So while that is waiting, you get married, you have kids, and that dream goes out the window, so. But as much as that goes out the window, your skill remains with you. So right now, I play at a league in Germantown, uh, it's called, uh, the, uh—I forgot it again—it's a semiprofessional league, there's a **soccerplex** in Germantown, uh, WISL, Washington International Soccer League, so we play Sunday games and then Saturday we practice.

7. FLYING

MAN: Entertainment. I'm not a big television person. I-I, TV has its place but . . . movies. I-I love music, I'd have to say, and I-I play piano. My wife is a pianist as well. I also play the flute. Um, years ago, as a kid, I played the violin, viola, and trumpet, and so music is very important to me. Uh, we, I don't get out to concerts much but mostly I'm at home just either listening to music, playing music, uh, not so much watching movies but just enjoying, enjoying life. Uh, I also am a federal, I guess a **licensed pilot**. I've been flying for about, since 1998, so about nine years, **instrument-rated pilot**, and now that I've recently returned to freelancing, uh, in my private practice as an interpreter, I should have more time to fly, so it's one of things I'm looking forward to, is spending more time back in the air. Since I've moved to the area for the past year and a half, I've been going back to New Jersey and flying with the same, uh, **fixed-based operator, FBO**, that I was flying with out of New Jersey, and so now I hope to return to the skies a little bit more in this area.

INTERVIEWER: Where did you learn to fly?

MAN: At Teterboro, uh, Airport in New Jersey at a school called Airfleet Training Systems. And, uh, it was just a dream I always had and working for myself at the time, I had the time. I also started learning with a friend from kindergarten who always wanted to fly. I just think through our twenties, we didn't have the funds to learn how to fly, so finally at thirty, we both decided, "We'd better get started now before we get too old." And so we both started learning together at the same time, which is good, because once you're in the air, it's **kinda** lonely, if you're just going around with, you know, to different locations, it's exciting. But having a friend, someone there that you can fly with and split the cost with as well, has been exciting, so we kinda learned at the same time.

INTERVIEWER: Have you flown just in New Jersey or what's the farthest that you've flown?

MAN: The farthest I've flown would probably be from New Jersey to Maine. It's **not terribly far**. But I've-I've flown from New Jersey to the Maryland area, uh, to Virginia, but I think the farthest would be to Maine, so just a couple of hours, two to three hours.

8. OUTDOORS IN NEW ZEALAND

Well, um, compared to here, you see, I have a little boy myself now and he's eight years old, so I remember my own childhood at the age of eight very often because you relive it. You know, if you've never had a child before and you get to reexperience everything of your own. The difference was, I think, in New Zealand, you can't understate how much the outdoors plays a role in life. Uh, as, and-and the United States is an outdoors country, too, but New Zealand is filled with, um, with beautiful things and a temperate climate, and New Zealanders by culture love sport, obsessively, uh, I would say. Y'know, you think it's-it's obsessive here; i-it's not, comparatively. And so, people, and that's why you get some of these very unusual sports being developed there, like people jumping off bridges and, uh, and bouncing and **bungee jumping** and throwing themselves against things, you know, all that. It comes from a love of doing things like that. And so, uh, childhood there, um, memories of-of-of being involved in the outdoors and-and, uh, and playing, but mostly making your own entertainment. Um, it's not a structured environment. People forge their own, uh, their own games, their own ideas. When you go for the summer holidays, you're usually off on an adventure somewhere, you know. It's, uh, yeah, that, so those-those spring to mind.

9. WALLYBALL

MAN: Uh, I like to play sports. I like to drive my Jeep, um, go **four-wheeling**. Um, I guess mess around with the computer, a few things.

INTERVIEWER: What kind of sports do you like to play?

MAN: Uh, I played soccer for about four years. I was a goalie. I played lacrosse for two years—I was still goalie. I'm very, I have that catlike reflex even though it doesn't look like it 'cause of my size. Uh, I play a sport called wallyball. It's volleyball and handball mixed in together, but instead of playing volleyball outside, it's indoors in a small court, and you can use the wall to bounce the ball off of. You just can't touch the ceiling or you can't touch two walls at the same time and you still use the ground to score on. Like, I play with kids my age on one team and fifty-year-old guys on the other team. So far, that, we barely ever beat 'em, so far, the old guys.

INTERVIEWER: So how many people are on a team?

MAN: Um, it depends on how many people show up that night. I mean, it could be three, three on three, it could be two on two, it could be, uh, up to three teams of four.

INTERVIEWER: Do you have, do you play in a league or just **pickup games**?

MAN: It's more of like, I play with my girlfriend's dad and just—it's more of like people we know throughout, uh, businesses and stuff, and friends.

10. MAKING MOVIES

MAN: Um, when I can manage some time, uh, I always have believed in-in, uh, being industrious. I try not to limit myself to just nursing or business. I find time to, uh, to showcase or act in some movies, if that's possible. I also did modeling, uh, in my day, and, uh, and it is my aspiration to end up on the big screen one day in Hollywood. So this is just a movie that actually, uh, was released today. Uh, it's called *Through the Fire*. It's, uh, a

Nigerian-based movie, uh, and then, uh, it just tells the story of how people leave Africa and come here and go through what they go through to get, uh, **status** adjusted or to get health care if they're out of status and stuff like that. Just the struggles that Africans go through when they come to America.

INTERVIEWER: How many movies have you made or how much acting have you done since you've been here?

MAN: Acting—actually, since I came to this country, this is the second movie, uh, that I'm in. Uh, when I used to be back home, uh, we did a lot more stage drama at the university. I was actually the theatrical director for one of the groups at the university, so I was exposed in that way, so when I came, I did not want to let, uh, my acting, uh, ambition and aspirations, uh, go to waste.

11. LIFE-WORK BALANCE

Uh, I keep **pretty busy**, I guess, um. I don't, uh, I'm not one of these people that have a billion hobbies, uh, I mean, I know, there's people like my dad who always has, you know, **spelunking** and, you know, whatever else that he's learning—sailing—and doing. He always has a-a thousand things to do with, uh, all of this, um. But I-I keep pretty busy. I'm-I'm somebody that likes to keep a very good life-work balance so I-I'm not sitting in the office for eighty hours a week, uh, but I'm married and I spend, we spend a lot of time together, uh. We do different things. This is—well, this is baseball season, although it's too cold. But, uh, so this time of year, there's, baseball just started, which gets us all excited. Um, what else do we do? We love to travel, uh, and that's, uh, that's, we're getting ready for a trip right now.

12. PLAYING THE PIANO

MAN: Depends on the mood. I would say, uh. I-I play some religious music, some **spiritual music**. A lot of, some, I-I guess my wife would call them show tunes, and it's probably with the influence from theater, but just a lot of, uh, anything that I interpret, I have to get the music because it's a work expense, and I need to be familiar with how to interpret the music, and so I have lots of music, uh, in my library. And so there-there, lots of show tunes, lots of, uh, spiritual music, some jazz, some **classical music**—that's pretty much it.

INTERVIEWER: When do you play?

MAN: Pretty much every Sunday. It's, there's, there're two things that I do on Sunday and it's, this is just what's happened over the years. I typically play at least a song or two towards the evening, and I also watch "Animal Planet." And so it's just, uh, a habit that my wife has gotten, she and I have gotten into before we had kids. It's just a calming thing, it's a Sunday evening, it's relaxing, "Let's look at the animals," and it's just become a tradition in that my daughter and I have now started Sunday evening, "It's time to watch 'Animal Planet,'" and we . . . The-the question was, "When do . . . ?" When do I play—so Sunday evening, I'd say, uh, pretty much. And any other time that I have a **free moment**. The other time I play is when I'm waiting for my wife, uh, when we're about to go out. She's, I'm always ready first and the kids are ready and we're always waiting, and so in that-that little **span of time** where we're waiting for my wife to finish getting ready before we depart to go out, I usually play a song or two just to pass the time.

13. THE **PERFORMING ARTS**

WOMAN: I go to a lot of plays, um, at both the Studio The-atre—**season tickets** there—and the Shakespeare The-atre. And I, um, went there after I saw *The Trojan Women.* I'm like so-so on Shakespeare—I like Shakespeare, I like Greek tragedy a lot, um, and it's, so, the combination is interesting. Uh, Studio Theatre has interesting, you know, sort of newer things to see; occasionally the Arena Stage, um, I'll go to. Movies I like. Um, some dance things, you know, I like, and concerts, um . . .

INTERVIEWER: What was the last concert you saw?

WOMAN: Last concert I saw was Yo-Yo Ma and the Silk Road, which I thought was really, uh, interesting, yeah, so.

INTERVIEWER: So classical music?

WOMAN: Yeah, I like classical, I like modern sort of, um, something called Trip-Hop, which is kind of jazzy, it's English. I don't know, it's not really rock but electron-ica—kind of that, um, so I do that. I'm not much of a tele-vision watcher. Occasionally, and I've taken up **knitting**. I'm learning how to knit. And so, it's too boring to do it by itself, so, like, Jon Stewart, I can watch Jon Stewart, I-I watch Jon—I like him a lot. He's funny, so a little bit of that and I'll knit and . . .

INTERVIEWER: What inspired the learning how to knit?

WOMAN: Um, there's a woman in my office who's an expert **knitter** and she offered to teach people how to knit, and I said, "Oh, what the heck?" you know. And um, Thurs-day at lunch, you can go in and knit and, um, talk with people, learn how to do new things, so. My mother is still shocked, shocked. She-she can't believe it, so.

14. BOOKS ON TAPE

I do, um, I do read. Uh, I-I don't read nearly as much as other people. I know my wife devours b—, you know, paperbacks like there's no tomorrow. Uh, but I always have a book on tape that I listen to, which I consider reading, uh, but I always, I always have a book on tape that I'm listening to, to and from work. Uh, my commute to work is about, uh, thirty-five to forty minutes, um, and I, and then I also always have a book that I'm actually reading, which is mostly for the days I'm on public transit. And, uh, right now I'm reading—what am I reading? It's a book about Venice, of course, because I'm getting ready for my trip. Uh, I forget what it's called—*City of Fallen Angels*? Uh, so it's a little bit disorienting because I always have two—one in my car and one that I'm reading—and then there's also the fact that my, we have two cars and a driveway that, you know, whoever comes in last is the car that's available. One car has a CD player and the other car has a tape player, so I always have one that I'm reading, one that I'm listening to on cassette, and one that I'm listening to on CD. Um, but, and then in, what I listen to usually rotates between a fiction and a history. Uh, the public library has a fabulous collection of books and CDs of college courses and history, and it's a lot of stuff that, you wouldn't necessarily pick up and read a biography of Julius Caesar but, you know, listening to and from work, it's fabulous—or the travels of Marco Polo, to and from work. It's not necessarily something I'm gonna pick up and read on a Saturday afternoon, but—so I do a lot of that.

15. READING

MAN: Reading. I do a lot of reading. I have three book-cases in the house full of books.

INTERVIEWER: What sorts of things do you read?

MAN: Everything. You name it. I probably have a book on everything, how to do everything. And I'm particularly interested in World War II, and especially the airborne units of World War II, and what they did and that type of thing. But military history in general, like Civil War, First World War, World War II—all the way up.

16. OPERA

You know that, you know, you often ask yourself the-the moon question: what beer do you bring to the moon? Or-or what, or-or-or what, uh, or-or, who, what music do you bring to the moon? You know, uh, the beer would have to be Guinness because it's good for every occasion, although I love **Natty Boh**, uh, because it's a hot-weather beer—we live in hot weather, uh, but, um, what? I've often asked myself that question and-and-and, um. Well, a couple years ago—it changes day to day—right now, you're asking me, uh, there's on—, there's three. I mean, there's Mozart, but Mozart, you have to be absolutely—Mozart is frenetic, he can be frenetic, he-he-he demands a lot of you. Uh, Verdi, he'll just sweep you, he'll just sweep you away but sometimes it, um, sometimes you don't want to be swept away, sometimes it's too many choruses, too much orchestra. Puccini, Puccini if you, if you, if you **wanna** cry, Puccini, or-or, in-in-in Verdi, especially in, uh, *Il Trovatore*, you know, the-the, uh, "*è pieno, è pieno, è pieno il mio cuor,*" you know, I-I-I . . . Or, uh, and then sometimes, on a, today was a French day because it's-it's-it's a C major day and sometimes, if-if the moon were, uh, in-in November or something. Dark. November day. Wind out there, some rain like yesterday—it has to be Wagner. It has to be Wagner. It has to be. It has to be the *Götterdämmerung*. It has to be, it has to be Brunhilde gettin' on Grane and going into the, into the fire. So-so-so actually, uh, if you ask me my moon, my moon, my moon opera, my moon composer . . . Who-who combines all three of those if you, if you really need it. Uh, I think right now, God sends me to the moon right now, I'd have to do Guinness, 'cause it's cold up there, and I'd have to do Verdi, because he's so universal.

17. PLAYING POOL

WOMAN: I go to the zoo.

MAN: She, weekends.

WOMAN: I go to the zoo, yeah.

INTERVIEWER: [OK, so we got that . . .]

MAN: Uh, skydive. Um, in my free time.

WOMAN: Well, we like to travel, [we like to go different places.

MAN: We do. We] like to travel, we like to **keep it going**. I occasionally drink a beverage. Just sort of something to do. I play pool. I play **pool** quite a bit. Um, what else [do we do]?

WOMAN: [Jigsaw puzzle.] We're working on a **jigsaw puzzle**.

MAN: We're **homebodies**, now that I think about it. We like to travel, but we're really homebodies.

INTERVIEWER: When do you play pool?

MAN: Ah, I usually play pool on Thursday nights in a APA league, American Pool Players Association, uh. It's, um, they, it becomes on a natio—, it-it can get to a national level. It's starts at a very local, your own—your home bar, you know, sort of thing. Uh, they have some really **scrappy** nasty tables and constantly smoke-filled rooms and you play there. And you go t—, at the end of session you can go to, uh, um, a tournament, which is your little area, which might be five bars in the neighborhood, uh, and if you win that you go to, uh, uh, sort a local, uh, meeting for districts, and districts can be all over the state, uh, and that's usually played, which was five minutes from her old house. Um, we, after that point, if you actually win that and you become champions in **eight ball** in that tier for the state, they, at that juncture, will pay for you and your eight team members' plane tickets to Las Vegas, and, uh, they put you up in a hotel out there, and you go to a national tournament out there.

WOMAN: He's never made it that far.

MAN: We've never made it that far. I've known people who've gone to Vegas, that they've gotten flown to Vegas, but our, any team that I've ever been on has-has not gone that far. Even if you win a few rounds of the, uh, national things that are happening locally, ra—, actually, not national, at the state level, um, they will pay you. We-we've gotten a payout of our team members, each one, somewhere in the neighborhood of forty or fifty dollars, which is actually very good. It's, you're at least winning something at that point.

18. HOBBIES

MAN: Hmm, I got all kinds of hobbies. Skydiving.

INTERVIEWER: OK.

MAN: Flying. Fishing. Hunting. Uh, competitive rifle and pistol shooting. Uh, **ham radio**. Um, wood carving. Um, probably a bunch I can't even think of right now.

INTERVIEWER: So with-with that many hobbies, how do you spend your time with them—do you participate in whichever one . . . ?

MAN: Well, the-the seasons have a lot to do with that. Like in summertime, I like to be fishing, uh, skydiving, and flying and the weather's good. Uh, shooting outdoors and all that business. Come wintertime, we're not jumping so much, so I might do more ham radio, uh, hunting in the wintertime, um, woodworking, doing stuff in-in the house. But I like, I like being outdoors more than I like being indoors.

Well, I always wanted to **jump**. And when I left Medstar—when I retired from there—I started teaching flying up here at Hanover, and that's how I met Jim and I started flying **jumpers**, and then I decided I was gonna do it, so my wife bought me one jump for a birthday present. She said, "You're just gonna do this once." I said, "Yeah, that's it." So here we are, several hundred jumps later, and I'm still at it. And since I started at age sixty, uh, you know, a lot of people wonder why I do that. They-they doubt my psychological stability because I jump out of airplanes.

INTERVIEWER: But you obviously enjoy it?

MAN: Oh, yeah. And you, I've met more nice people sky-diving, and, uh, I've, I mean, there was an **esprit de corps** with the state police because you're involved in a situation where you have to depend on each other a lot but skydiving is-is a stronger esprit de corps, esprit de corps to me than with the state police, just because of the people involved and you're doing a sport that's, you know, potentially dangerous, so everybody's sort of lookin' out for everybody, you know. It's like when you jump, you, in the plane, you're looking at another guy's equipment to see if maybe everything's hooked up alright, and the other guy's lookin' at your stuff, too, so you-you know, you're lookin' out for each other. And it's a sport that not too many people do—what, there's thirty thousand of us in the United States?

DEFINITIONS

All-American: A designation given to collegiate athletes in the United States who are among the best in their particular sport.

BASE jump (BASE jumping–Building Antenna Span Earth): A kind of skydiving in which the participant jumps from a fixed object on the ground instead of from an aircraft.

bungee jumping: Jumping from a fixed object above the ground, such as a bridge or crane, with an elastic cord attached to one's body that stops the person's descent after falling for some distance but before reaching the ground or water below.

'cause: Short for *because.*

classical music: Typically, music from the late eighteenth and early nineteenth centuries by European composers such as Beethoven, Mozart, Brahms, Wagner, Bach, and the like.

computer games: Interactive video games designed to be played on a computer.

dressage: An equestrian sport in which the rider guides the horse through a series of movements in a manner as relaxed and effortless as possible. The rider is judged on how well he or she performs the movements with the horse.

eight ball: A game in pocket billiards in which the object is for a player to sink all of the balls he or she is shooting before sinking the eight ball.

'em: Short for *them.*

esprit de corps: A French phrase meaning "camaraderie" or "team spirit."

fixed-based operator (FBO): A center at an airport that provides services such as parking, tie-down, fueling, and flight training for pilots and aircraft owners.

flat work: Movements or maneuvers that a rider on horseback guides the horse to perform while on level ground—the basis of dressage.

four-wheeling: A recreational activity that involves driving a motor vehicle specially designed for use in rugged off-road (not streets or highways) areas.

free moment: A brief period of time for which there is no obligation to do something.

full of himself: Egotistical, self-centered, stubborn, or arrogant.

goalie: Slang or short for *goalkeeper*. A defensive position in soccer (or hockey) whose sole purpose is to prevent the opposing team from scoring.

gonna: Going to.

ham radio: Amateur radio used as both a service and a hobby in which different kinds of radio equipment are used for communication to allow people at different locations in the world to communicate with each other. It is sometimes referred to as shortwave radio.

hang glide (hang gliding): An aerial sport in which the participant glides through the air while suspended beneath a wing-type glider made of fabric-type material covering a metal frame.

hang out: To spend time alone or with friends with no specific agenda in mind.

homebodies: People who like to stay at home, or people whose life is centered around the home.

instrument-rated pilot: A pilot who has received additional training, education, and certification that allow him or her to fly in conditions or situations that require the use of more specialized flight instrumentation for navigating and controlling an aircraft.

iPod: A small, portable electronic device on which music or other kinds of recordings can be stored and played back.

jigsaw puzzle: Typically, a large flat puzzle with some kind of pattern, picture, or design on it that takes a significant amount of time to assemble.

jump: A term often used synonymously with *skydiving.*

jumpers: Skydivers.

keep it going: To stay active or busy and participate in different activities.

kinda: Kind of.

knitter: A person who knits.

knitting: To make something from yarn or thread by using needles to produce interconnecting loops of material.

licensed pilot: A person who has met all of the training and educational requirements established by the FAA (Federal Aviation Administration) and who has been issued a permit to fly an aircraft.

MLS (Major League Soccer): The professional soccer league of North America.

MSI (Montgomery Soccer Incorporated): A local youth soccer league.

Natty Boh: Nickname for the American beer National Bohemian.

not terribly far: A common expression that means "not very far."

off the beaten path: Places to which people do not frequently go or travel.

outdoorsman: A person who enjoys outside sports or activities.

performing arts: Refers to live entertainment such as theater, ballet, and concerts.

pickup games: Informal games in which teams are formed in an impromptu fashion from the people that are available.

pool: A game or games similar to billiards but played on a table with pockets in which the object is to sink or pocket more balls, or certain balls, before your opponent does.

pretty busy: Very busy.

riding: Reference to horseback riding.

RV (recreational vehicle): A kind of motor vehicle in which people can live as they travel from place to place.

scrappy: Rough, ragged, or of poor quality.

scuba dive (SCUBA–Self-Contained Underwater Breathing Apparatus): A kind of diving in which a person carries his or her own air supply.

season tickets: Tickets that a person purchases for a specific kind of event that allows him or her to attend every scheduled performance that takes place during a specified period of time.

sign: To use sign language.

soccerplex: An arena where soccer is played.

span of time: A period of time.

spelunking: The sport of exploring caves.

spiritual music: Music with a religious theme.

status: Immigration status.

stopper: A defensive player in soccer who occupies a midfield position outside of the sweeper.

sweeper: A defensive player in soccer who occupies a position between the goalkeeper and the rest of the defensive line.

touristy: Something that is designed for, caters to, or appeals primarily to tourists.

wanna: Want to.

QUESTIONS AND EXERCISES

1. List the three most interesting pastimes described by the speakers and explain why you think they are interesting.

2. What role do pastimes play in the lives of these speakers?

3. Which pastime would you like to try and why?

4. Describe the pastimes of a friend, colleague, or classmate.

5. How much free time do you have? Are you able to balance free time and work?

6. Identify three words or phrases in this chapter that are new to you, and write a sentence with each one.

CHAPTER 7

THE USE OF LANGUAGE
PART I

In this chapter, interviewees talk about the role of language in their lives.

1. SOUNDING AMERICAN

I think that the most difficult thing for them to learn is actually, um—that's a good question. Well, if I were to get technical about it, I would say that pronunciation is the hardest thing to learn. I-I see people—I have a lot of contact with internationals just because my husband is a, is an international, my parents were, um. They have a tremendous facility with English in general, they can use

English in everyday communication, they use English in sort of very specialized areas, science or linguistics, and they're comfortable with that and they're very proficient, but they still maintain this accent, so I would say that sounding like an American on a phonological point, uh, level, of having the American accent, I think that's a lot harder than, um, mastering the grammar or even mastering some of the idiomatic phrases that sort of make you stand out as a, would normally make you sound like a native speaker but, um, the-the accent is sort of, is very tenacious.

I think I pay more attention to them, and I think it's because growing up I was very aware of, I wanted to sound like an American when I spoke English, but I wanted to sound like a Taiwanese when I spoke Taiwanese. And I had a Taiwanese accent speaking English in the beginning, and I was very, very, very determined to standardize that accent and make it sound like Middle America. So I-I-I do remember watching the news with my father and foll-following along underneath my voice, and on a soft voice, what the news anchor was saying, to try to mold my accent closer to his. And that was at a very young age, I was doing that, so that by the time I was twelve or thirteen, I had pretty much wiped out whatever Taiwanese accent I had. And by the time I was fifteen, I no longer had a Maine accent, so I was as standard as I could make my accent. On the Taiwanese side, I was, um, always upset when we would go to Taiwan and people would look at me and after three minutes of talking to me, say, "Oh, you must be an American, you-you came here from America." And that really, that really upset me, since Taiwanese was my native language, my first language—I didn't speak English until I was old enough to play with other children, um—but living in this country, with the exposure that I had, I-I had some vestigial American accent that people could always identify me.

I've worked on that, too, and really listened to understand why my pronunciation is different from my mother's or different from my aunt's, and as a result, I think actually my-my accent has improved as I've gotten older, but now they identify me with a much older cohort, I sound like I'm about fifty or sixty 'cause those are my models that I've, I-I speak like, um, but, yeah, all my life I've really tried to, I've been very aware of my accent and tried to modify it, um, not always successfully, with-with varying success depending on which language we're talking about, but that is always been something that's been very much at the front of my mind, so I'm very aware of that.

2. LINGUISTIC CHAMELEON

Considering that, as a, I grew up as a, as I said, as **Navy brat** and I lived in many different regions of the country growing up. Uh, sure, there're-there're definitely different accents. And a funny thing that I've noticed about myself, and I'm—somebody else observed it in me, I wasn't even consciously aware of it until somebody pointed it out—but I'm somewhat of a linguistic chameleon in that whatever accent I'm speaking with is usually, I-I'll gravitate towards the person that I'm speaking with, because I lived in so many different places and have adopted so many different accents, you know. If-if I'm speaking to somebody from the South, I'll—without even being consciously aware of it—I'll slide into a little bit of a **drawl** and-and-and it-it just is-is a very natural thing for me, whereas if I'm speaking to somebody from a more urban area, uh, or-or the West Coast, there's a li-little bit of an Oregon accent. It's hard for me to put my finger on but, uh, there're definitely regional differences, and because I've lived in so many different regions, I-I'll just kind of slide into that accent without even being conscious of it, when I'm speaking to somebody from those areas.

3. SPEAKING SPANISH

STUDENT: Um, I'm fluent in Spanish 'cause I was in the dual-language program when I was really little, like around six, so I remember in first grade, uh, my school taught me Spanish. And, um, I'm still in it now. I'm in a lot of **AP** classes, which are college courses in high school. And then, um, I kind of grew up at Gallaudet and, um, I know some sign language. I'd really, really like to learn more though, but I-I have an OK vocabulary.

INTERVIEWER: Do you have much occasion to use your Spanish?

STUDENT: Um, I have more than I would like to, um. My parents, every time we go to a restaurant or we just see anyone who's Hispanic, they make me talk to them and sometimes, I don't know, if I were in a foreign country, I don't think I would like someone going, "Oh, I speak English, talk to me!" You know? So, I feel like it's kind of mean. But they make me talk to people in Spanish all the time. Sometimes they like it, though, sometimes they like it because they can relate and it's nice to hear your own language. Sometimes maybe they're annoyed by it. I would be.

INTERVIEWER: Have you had a chance to go to Spanish-speaking countries and use it?

STUDENT: Yeah, in sixth grade I went to Spain for two weeks with my mom and my grandma and, uh, we traveled all around from Madrid to Barcelona to Sevilla and, um, it was, it was fun, although now that I look back, I was just kind of too young to go, but that actually helped me a lot—just two weeks made me so much more fluent than I already was.

4. LISTENING

MAN: It was hard, is not easy because you have to make your living while as you go to school at the same times. And back home, most, uh, students just go to school. They don't have to work to make the living. So it's little bit here, it's little bit stressful and hard to learn at the same time you have to make your living at the same times.

INTERVIEWER: So what would you say was the hardest thing ⌈about learning English⌉?

MAN: ⌊It's still, sometimes⌋ I have little bit heavy accent, uh, in my language, so I took some classes to imp—, to prove my accent so people can understand me a lot more better. But, uh, I learned, when you talk to the client, just slow down a little bit because when you speak fast like American people sometimes you don't get the point, so I slow down and try to explain it carefully so they, I make sure they got the point of what I'm trying to explain to-to him or to them.

INTERVIEWER: Do you have trouble understanding different accents in America?

MAN: Sometimes. From the South, sometimes, but I always listen, and if I don't understand, I ask again, they repeat what you said.

5. COLOR COMMENTARY

I know from what my mother has told me that I was a very late talker. Like not, she thought something was wrong. I wasn't saying anything, um, until one day I **busted out** with a whole sentence. Um, so she's like, "Oh, thank goodness, nothing's wrong." So I think that my daughter, Aida, is speaking much earlier than I ever did, and I think part of the reason is—well, part of the reason is she's the only child we have and I was number two, so that might have contributed—but in the, bigger component is the fact that she has all this sort of language stimulation all of the time, and she's constantly going back and forth, and she really gets it. Maybe she was just also genetically predisposed to being verbal, I don't know, but I think that sort of compilation of characteristics has made this **chatterbox**, which is what she is. I've, I-I think that she may become, um, a **play-by-play**, do **color commentary**, because that's what she does all day long: "OK, I'm sitting now, OK, let's go," and everything is, she does little commentary of everything that we're doing: "OK, we're sitting now. Now where are we going? We are going to the store." Everything . . .

6. GROWING UP BILINGUALLY

MAN: English—actually I grew up, uh, with English language. Uh, we were colonized by, uh, after the Second World War, at the end of the Second World War. Uh, Cameroon was one of the countries that was partitioned between Britain and France, and so it made us a de facto, uh, bilingual country. So, I grew in the English section, studied entirely in English. And, of course, we spoke the dialect at home, but when we went to school, we, uh, studied in English. But going to the university, to the university, we had to go to the French section. Uh, there's ten provinces in Cameroon. Eight of them are, uh, French speaking and two of them are English speaking, so you have to go to the French side to go to university, so then you're supposed to be bilingual, so we started studying French while going to primary school in the English section to prepare for university in the French section, so. Uh, English, I grew up learning English, but French I had to study as a second language.

INTERVIEWER: So, d'y—, do people comment on your accent?

MAN: At times, at times. Uh, when I came initially in '94, I might have had a little bit of a heavier accent. Uh, I don't know that it will ever change that much, but, uh, sometimes some people do not understand when I express myself, sometimes, but most often than not, uh, I articulate, I believe I articulate well because I studied linguistics also at the university. Not that that should matter, but somehow I put a lot of emphasis on my phonetics and pronunciation so a lot of people can get along with understanding me, but you run into occasions where, uh, people just cannot get what you say, and I would say something about two or three times, and they would be like, "What are you saying?" Then eventually when they get it, they really do not say it far from what I said, you know, so I said, "Maybe it's the accent," you know.

INTERVIEWER: Now do you have trouble understanding people in the United States who have different accents?

MAN: Not really. Um, I-I'm at a point now where I can actually tell sometimes if you're from the South or from California or from Vegas, you know, so I not only understand what they say but I can decipher, uh, which section they-they coming from, but every now and then, you run into somebody that have a very fast speech, you know, very rapid speech, and it's hard to pick up everything they say. And, uh, it's not too difficult understanding people in the United States because also the choice of words. They use high-frequency words, uh. By high-frequency words, words you hear every day, you know, it's, uh, when you start reading a book, uh, like Agatha Christie or something, then you see words which could be challenging or require you to go into the dictionary to see what they mean. But in everyday language, uh, a lot of Americans—and this is probably a plus—use, uh, high-frequency words, so there is no mystery in the language, **so to speak**.

7. GETTING COMFORTABLE

WOMAN: Um, well, I think that, um, one of the hardest things, um, for learning any foreign language is, uh, just becoming comfortable with yourself in that language. Um, and, uh, so, for example, pronunciation for me, uh, one of the, I think I'll always have an ac—, a foreign accent in English, no matter how many years I live here, and you have to feel comfortable with that, OK? I have a foreign accent and that's just me, that's just part of me, part of who I am, and you have to reach a point at which you feel comfortable, comfortable with that and not, uh, self-conscious about it. So that's one of the hardest things.

Now, if we go to the specifics, uh, I think that one of the things that everybody complains about when they're learning English is all these preposition—I think they call them particle verbs—these prepositional verbs like, uh, **turn up, turn out, turn in**. Everybody gets confused about those, uh, and if you get the wrong preposition, of course, you're saying the wrong thing. So I think that's a hard thing because it's very idiomatic, and, of course, the most idiomatic aspects of the language are the ones that are harder to learn. You just have to get immersed in the culture and just pick them up.

I have trouble with, uh, the accents-accents from, uh, the South of the United States, uh, 'cause, I mean, if, I think I can travel anywhere in the Northeast and even though there are different accents, I don't think I have problems understanding people in general. Um, I've lived in the Northwest and in the Southwest, and I never had any trouble, but when I lived in North Carolina, when I first moved to North Carolina, I could not understand my own students. I mean, I had trouble with the southern accent and then, of course, I got used to it. But, uh, yeah, in terms of geographical accents, I would say the southern accent.

INTERVIEWER: So what did you do when you couldn't understand somebody?

WOMAN: I asked them to repeat or I, or I just guessed.

DEFINITIONS

AP: Advanced placement classes, offered in high school.

busted out: In this context, to have suddenly exclaimed or to have said something unexpectedly.

'cause: Short for *because.*

chatterbox: Slang for a talkative person.

color commentary: Information provided by one of the members of a broadcast team at a sporting event that is designed to fill time when action is not taking place in the competition. That information includes things such as personal interest stories, statistics, and points of strategy.

drawl: A colloquial word used to describe the lengthening of vowels in a person's speech. It is frequently found in speech patterns in the southern United States.

linguistic chameleon: A person who adapts or adjusts his or her speech and language usage to match the environment in which he or she is at any given time.

Navy brat: A child who grew up with one or both parents in the U.S. Navy and typically lived in many places.

play-by-play: A detailed moment-to-moment description of the action in a sporting event.

so to speak: A phrase used to mean "as an example" or "in that way."

turn in: Often used to mean "go to bed."

turn out: The end or resolution of a situation—for example, "How did everything turn out?" It can also mean the attendance of people at an event.

turn up: To appear or become available.

QUESTIONS AND EXERCISES

1. What do these speakers think about accents?

2. What do you notice about accents?

3. In your experience, what is the hardest thing about learning English?

4. Do you speak differently, depending on whom you are talking to?

5. How many languages do you speak? When and how did you learn them?

6. Identify three words or phrases in this chapter that are new to you, and write a sentence with each one.

CHAPTER 8

THE USE OF LANGUAGE PART II

In this chapter, interviewees continue to share their perspectives on the role of language in their lives.

1. AMERICAN ENGLISH/BRITISH ENGLISH

MAN: I, of course, since, India is, we have been ruled by Britishers, so I know English pretty well. And, uh, I know In—, few Indian languages. I mean, like one of them is, uh, Hindi, and I also know, uh, Punjabi—that's-that's where, uh, my family belongs to, Punjab, the north part of India—and a little bit of Urdu.

INTERVIEWER: Uh-hmm. So in which situations do you use your, [your languages]?

MAN: [If-if I have an Indian] client and I know that he speaks Hindi, to make that person comfortable, I speak Hindi. It's all what kind of client I have. I mean, there's some clients who may be from India, origin from India, but they hesitate speaking an Indian language, so I-I don't mind. It's all **customer service**, so. Whosoever feels comfortable, whatever.

INTERVIEWER: So even with Indian clients, you may speak English?

MAN: Yes, yes. I mean, like the, some of the Indian, regions in India, they do not speak Hindi. If you go to south, they speak southern language and English. So by and large, English is kind of language that is easily understood by most of the people, like, unless you go into the suburban areas of India, so, you know, you'll have a problem with English, but otherwise, most people speak English. So it's either Hindi or English, but when I have people from, uh, northern part of India, which is called Punjab, so I-I speak in Punjabi, and they-they are thrilled about it. I mean, they feel pretty much at home.

Oh, you mean in America, yes. Uh, I mean, I find it, uh, I have to struggle to make people understand what I'm saying because I-I speak mostly British English and it's not exactly British accent, it's British English. Uh, but in America also I find that I-I went to Florida with my son for vacation, so it's like you could see that, they speak differently. And the, some of the words they don't use and some of the words they use, we never use it here, so. I mean, they-they could tell that, "Oh, we-we, you're not from Florida, right?" So I-I know that they can make out that I am, definitely I am not from America, so they can make out. But when they even speak to my son, who speaks very good American English, as for the standard of Maryland, even he could be distinguished that he's not from Florida, so I-I definitely notice this. But, of course, I've not traveled so much so I can't say **for sure**.

INTERVIEWER: What about, I mean, when you lived in New York or in other places—do you, do you have a hard time understanding accents or . . . ?

MAN: Uh, no. I never had a problem to understand what they're saying, but **by and large**, there's some kind of people, when they speak, they neither speak English nor they speak, I mean, I don't know if it's a different kind of language altogether. They are not pronouncing the words should be pronounced, so half of the time, it's like a **rap**, you have to try to understand the song, so when I was in-in-in, uh, in America, uh, in New York, I-I ha—, I had a hard time trying to follow. I mean, it's like, uh, you heard something, you have a pic—, like you have a picture memory, and then you try to figure out, "Oh, he meant, oh yeah, he said that." So, you can't, I'm, I was not very responsive, saying, "Oh, you're saying this" or "I'm saying this." So it's like, uh, "OK, he said that, yeah," eventually. You know, like when my boss, who was an American, he asked me, I said, "Uh, about that travel agent"—uh, because you're a wholesaler, about that travel agent—he said, "What about it?" "What about it?" is a very rude word in India. I mean, if I say "What about it?" that means I am saying, "What the hell you talking about?" You know, but what he meant was, "Tell me quickly what happened," OK, so that he can give a decision, so he was pretty normal. But I thought, "Why did he say that? I was only thinking about him." Then over a period of time, I realized he always says that, "What about it?" So, yeah, New York is too fast.

Uh, when they are learning English, I think the hardest part is, uh, I think everybody is confused whether they should learn the language English or they should understand the cul—, English culture here, because, um, anybody who migrates from their own country to here, there is lot of adjustments that you—the food adjustments, food habits, the way you work, the time you offer, dedication—you-you have to forget about basically. You have to **wipe the slate off completely**. So on top of it, if you have to learn English, then you're trying to understand the culture and the language. And, of course, English language by itself is very confused sometimes. When you put English English and American English, so there are some words like in India we say, "Uh, I need a, uh, I need a **torch**." So the torch in India is battery here, so, uh, if I tell somebody, "I need a torch," they say, "Why, do you want to bring my building down? You burn it down. Do you need a torch, fire?" So-so, they, so, it's like, uh, I mean, I had to learn, relearn English in American culture, so it's a culture and English both put together, sometimes can be **pretty intimidating**, yeah.

2. BALTIMORE

WOMAN: Some people say I sound like I'm from Boston, uh, which I've only visited, on-on occasion.

MAN: Did we go?

WOMAN: We drove through it.

MAN: We drove through it, right.

WOMAN: Um, we, some people say—let me see, there was another one. Recently someone asked me if I was, if I was—I-I don't want to say **Amish**, but it was something like that, and I can't think of what it was, but, um, maybe it was **Mennonite** or something. . . .

MAN: Oh, yeah.

WOMAN: Someone said I had a Mennonite accent, and, of course, I don't—I don't hear an accent at all. So, I'm like, "Nope." But I guess my accent would be from—it's more a dialect—but it would be from Highlandtown 'cause I grew up in the, in the city, in east Baltimore.

MAN: And just-just the way she says that, I say it differently. I say Highlandtown and, which you can tell that there's, but everybody has an accent.

WOMAN: Yeah, like-like ⎡ water-water ⎤.

MAN: ⎣So the question is, "Do⎦ you have an accent?" "**Yeahbsolutely**!"

WOMAN: So, I think it's a, more a dialect.

MAN: Right, it's . . .

INTERVIEWER: What about you? Do people tell you . . . ?

MAN: Um.

INTERVIEWER: Or how would you describe your accent?

MAN: Yes. And I, people have said something to me and, um, you'll obviously notice that if you, all you need to do is live somewhere else for any extended period of time and even where we're going, we'll probably get that. But, um, the, earlier, when I was very young and one of the first trips I took out west was to Denver, and I was skiing with a friend, and they asked me where I was from. I said, "Baltimore." And he said, "Balmore? Balmore? Baldwin? Bal? Balmore?" They didn't know what I was saying. I said, "I'm from Baltimore." He said, "What-what's Baltimore?" I s—, I said, "Uh, the Orioles play there." And they go, "Oh, you mean Bal-ti-more." "Yeah." "Oh, yeah, Balmore, Baltimore, yes." That's what they . . . So, yeah, of

course, we have accents. I-I call that an accent. Probably
is a dialect. Is that the right word, I think?

INTERVIEWER: Do you, do you notice accents in the other,
in other parts of the country?

WOMAN: Yeah, that's the, that's the joy of the United
States, is that, you know, people don't talk the same. Uh,
you know, it all, it's all different. I mean, we have the
mountains and the water and the valleys in between. I
mean, it's like we have everything—like many different
countries all in, all in one, ⌈and I do⌉ . . .

MAN: ⌊What is?⌋

WOMAN: The United States. I do en—, so I do enjoy listening to other people talk, like, I mean, if you talk to anybody from the **Bronx**, you definitely know they're from
the Bronx, uh . . .

MAN: Boston.

WOMAN: Boston—you definitely know they're from . . .

MAN: Boston.

WOMAN: Boston. So that's the joy of being in the United
States and traveling in the United States. You get many
more cultures in a much more contained free area where
you can just go to easily. You don't even need a passport.

MAN: And some people look at you funny.

WOMAN: Yeah.

3. A FRENCH-CANADIAN PERSPECTIVE

WOMAN: Well, I haven't been exposed much to Texas and
Deep South accents, but the few times that I have heard

those accents, I did struggle a bit, yes. Um, Quebec has different accents, even just in the French that is being spoken up there, and that-that's very interesting 'cause I have met lots of people down here that come from Quebec, and we can tell which area we're from just from the way we speak our French and I-I had learned English in school in Montreal, but I could barely speak a full sentence when I got here in Baltimore for school, so basically I learned to speak English here, and I can recognize all the different accents—English accents that are like being, you know, that I hear around me—but I guess my ears are better than, you know, my mouth, like, me, as far as like perfecting the way I speak English is a lot harder than me, like, recognizing all the other accents going on around me.

What was the hardest for me was to be in a very big group of people speaking very fast. Um, the hardest thing . . . I guess, I-I don't know . . . the hardest thing. I guess it would be to just get used to the vocabulary, because the verbs in English, you know, no matter how they are used, whether it's, like, future, past, or present tense, they always look or sound about the same. But the vocabulary is just so vast and luckily, going from French to English, lots of the words are similar, just pronounce them differently, but I guess personally, I had, my-my biggest struggle was the spoken part. I could read fine, I could write paper—it would take me a long time, but I could write my papers—but the dialogue part . . .

MAN: I don't doubt that part of that was complicated by the fact that nobody in America actually speaks proper English.

4. WHERE ARE YOU FROM?

Um, well, my accent has picked up little things from different places that I've been. I would describe it as, it's very hard when you're, uh, going to a new place, and as I said, you know, I traveled all to those different countries trying to sell my TV show, and it was a real challenge. This was probably the easiest place in terms of the-the people in business are welcoming here. Um, whereas Europe is, from my perspective—from my experience—doesn't like to experiment too much with new things. Um, in, uh, in the U.S., they love it, that is what they-they want and their motivation. So I would be faced with having to talk to people most of the time who didn't want to talk to me. So having an accent that was slightly different meant I got another minute or two that they listened to me, before they got rid of me. So in that way, in that way, my accent, um, helped. Where they, most people, it depends where you are, where they think you're from. Um, if you're, if I was in England, they would, they'd be sure I was a colonial and they would say so. If I was here, uh, if I were in the U.S., they would probably think I was Australian or South African or-or English. Um, when I'm

in New Zealand, now they're not sure where I am from. They, you know, but, "I'm from right here." Uh, when I'm there, I say that. So-so it depends where you are.

5. CHANGE OVER TIME

Yes, most people will ask me where I'm from, in the United States. Uh, I think it's funny, though, when I go back to England and if I used a British passport or they looked carefully at my American passport, they'd say, "Welcome home." But everybody would call me a **Yank**. Uh, so to a **Brit**, no, they don't think I have an accent other than maybe an American accent. In the United States, most people think I have an accent. Uh, probably less and less people think it's British, just because of time.

6. A CARIBBEAN PERSPECTIVE

WOMAN: Yes, and they keep wondering, "After forty-something years, you still have your accent?" I said, "Yes, I guess it's a part of me, so . . ."

INTERVIEWER: And what-what, how do you describe it to them? Your accent, I mean, when they say, "What-what kind of accent do you have?" What do you tell them?

WOMAN: A West Indian accent, it's a West Indian accent. Mm-hmm.

INTERVIEWER: Do you have trouble understanding accents in the United States, other accents?

WOMAN: Funny enough, not really, no, no. I always liked languages so, you know, and with, especially with Spanish, you had to learn the different accents or dialects, you know. So, no, I don't have any trouble with that, no.

INTERVIEWER: Do you al—, do you speak, uh, **Guyanese Creole** also?

WOMAN: ⌈No, no, mm-mm.⌉

INTERVIEWER: ⌊ No, you don't. ⌋You speak . . .

WOMAN: I just speak ⌈English⌉.

INTERVIEWER: ⌊English.⌋

WOMAN: English, mm-hmm.

INTERVIEWER: Do you understand it?

WOMAN: I understand **Pidgin Creole**.

INTERVIEWER: Right.

WOMAN: Yes, yes.

INTERVIEWER: Yes, so you do.

WOMAN: A little bit, yeah, mm-hmm.

INTERVIEWER: And did your family speak that when you were . . . ?

WOMAN: No, no. Strictly . . .

INTERVIEWER: No. Just strictly English.

WOMAN: Mm-hmm, mm-hmm. Yeah, you would, you would find people really in the country, those are the ones that would speak that, and the **Amerindians**, those are the ones that would speak that-that Creole language, but no.

INTERVIEWER: Do you hear differences between your accent and other accents in the Caribbean?

WOMAN: Yes, oh yes.

INTERVIEWER: For example . . .

WOMAN: Uh, Barbadians. Oh, you could tell the Barbadian accent, it's, uh, I don't know how to describe it, but you could tell that Barbadian accent. The Jamaican accent is also different. But the Guyanese, we roll our *r*s when you're speakin' so people say that they could always tell a Guyanese by the way the *r*s come out. Um, the Trinidadians, they have a singsong kind of way that they speak, so, yeah, you could tell the difference.

7. A SOUTHERN ACCENT

MAN: Yes, very.

INTERVIEWER: What kind of accent?

MAN: Well, I grew up in Arkansas, and so I do have, uh, influence of the South in-in my, in my speech. I left Arkansas after high school, however, and so for, since high school, I've lived on the **eastern seaboard**, and so the strength of the southern accent in my voice has diminished considerably. Uh, I find myself sort of in a, in an intermediate position now with recognition of my accent because when I live here on the East Coast, uh, people'll say things like, "You're not from around here, are you?" because they detect that trace of southern accent still in my, in my diction. But when I go back to visit friends in Arkansas, I've lived on the eastern seaboard long enough so that they tell me that I sound like I'm a damn **Yankee**.

INTERVIEWER: No kidding!

MAN: Oh yeah, yeah. They say . . .

INTERVIEWER: But you went to graduate school in North Carolina?

MAN: North Carolina—still the South, true, uh, still, certainly North Carolina has very strong southern, uh, dialect—but I've lived in D.C. now for almost thirteen years. . . .

INTERVIEWER: Right.

MAN: Um, and also I'll admit I have, I have intentionally tried to lose some of the, uh, stronger elements of my southern accent.

INTERVIEWER: ⌈   Like?   ⌉

MAN: ⌊Intentionally tried to.⌋ Um, well, I, uh, I prefer not to pronounce words the way they tend to be pronounced in Arkansas sometimes. For, an example is, uh, is the verb *going*, *g-o-i-n-g*. In Arkansas, it's slurred into a long diphthong frequently, and many people pronounce it "goeeng" as if it were the s—, you know, uh, yeah, pronounce it "goeeng." And I prefer to pronounce it "going," and so I've made an intentional effort now to say "going" rather than "goeeng."

INTERVIEWER: Right.

8. LANGUAGE AND CULTURE

The hardest thing? Um, the hardest thing, I would say, the hardest thing in-in-in America, to learn English— American English—would be to, uh, um, assume a love for the culture. Now, that may be difficult coming from, say, Italy-Ita, it-it-it may be difficult, and it's been difficult for every immigrant over here to assume a love for the culture that you have all of a sudden moved into and-and-and must-must-must assume the culture, but you have to have that, you have to have a love for it. If you don't have a love for it—I mean, you can have a practical reason for coming over. My-my-my grandparents did from Ireland, which, another language I've-I've studied, um, or-or my great-grandparents from Poland, uh, maybe-maybe have a reason for coming over here 'cause it-it wasn't **cool** over in Poland and it certainly wasn't cool over in Ireland—um, but, even-even about ten years ago, I-I could speak to my great-uncles that Lidia found through gea—, uh, uh, uh, genealogy, and, uh, they still spoke with-with-with an accent. They still spoke, uh, *polova populsku*, half Polish and-and it's in Chicago and-and-and, I-I-I, they, I-I don't assume that they-they-they, acquired a love for this culture and that may be difficult, coming from-from an-another—I'm not **gonna** say—we don't have a **hell of a lot** of culture, but it-it may be even a little more difficult for them to pick up coming over here than for us to pick up going over-over there.

DEFINITIONS

Amerindians: Indian people indigenous to the Americas and the Caribbean region.

Amish: A Christian religious sect of Swiss origin often found in eastern Pennsylvania and known for their choice not to use modern conveniences and modes of transportation.

Brit: Short for *British*.

Bronx: One of the five boroughs of New York City.

by and large: An expression that means "generally speaking," "for the most part," or "in most cases."

'cause: Short for *because*.

cool: A slang expression that means "to be desired or desirable," "to be with it," "to be in vogue," or "to be happening."

customer service: In business, addressing and meeting the needs of the customers or clients.

eastern seaboard: The eastern portion of the United States along the Atlantic Ocean.

for sure: With certainty.

gonna: Going to.

Guyanese Creole: A Creole language spoken by the people of Guyana.

hell of a lot: A slang expression that means "a large quantity."

Mennonite: A Christian religious sect devoted to peace from which the Amish are derived.

no kidding: An expression that means "Really? Is that true?"

Pidgin Creole: A layperson's term for a dialect spoken in Guyana. *Pidgins* are defined as languages that arise out of contact and that are no one's native language; *creoles* typically refer to pidgins that have native speakers—that is, the children of the speakers who originated the pidgin. Pidgins and creoles differ in linguistic structure.

pretty intimidating: Very intimidating.

rap: A kind of music in which the lyrics are spoken in a rhythmic fashion.

torch: In British English, a flashlight or some other kind of handheld light.

wipe the slate off completely (usually **wipe the slate clean**): To dismiss or disregard previous results or actions.

Yank, Yankee: A term often used by foreigners, usually Europeans, to refer to Americans.

yeahbsolutely: This speaker's combination of the words *yeah* and *absolutely*. An emphatic "yes."

QUESTIONS AND EXERCISES

1. Summarize what these speakers say about accents in the United States.

2. Do you have trouble understanding accents? If so, which ones and why?

3. Do people say that you have an accent? If so, how would you describe it?

4. Of the speakers in Chapter 7 and this chapter, which one has the accent that is the hardest to understand?

5. In your daily life, which accent is the most difficult to understand?

6. Identify three words or phrases in this chapter that are new to you, and write a sentence with each one.

CHAPTER 9

FOOD

In this chapter, interviewees talk about their favorite foods and about cooking.

1. COOKING VACATIONS

WOMAN: Well, I have found that-that a very interesting way to learn about the culture of a country is to go to that country and spend time with-with the people who-who create the food that people eat in those places. And, um, there's, there're a lot of opportunities in all kinds of, all parts of the world these days to travel, to go to areas that are sort out of the normal places that people, tourists go, um, but, uh, to go with small groups of people and meet chefs, meet home cooks, learn from them the things that are important to them in terms of how they cook, the traditions that they have, the kinds of ingredients that they use, and it really, really gives you, um, a real **eye-opening** lesson in what a real culture is like—very different from reading about it in a book or a magazine. (I) mean, the best thing would be to go and live in a place for a long time, but some of these sorts of experiences, you really get to meet people who are very passionate about the things that they do in their everyday life. And food is something that, I think, is worth having a great passion about.

INTERVIEWER: Where have you been on some of these cooking vacations?

WOMAN: Well, I've been a number of different places here in the United States. Um, (I've) been to New Mexico, for example, uh, California, uh, but I really have enjoyed traveling in Europe in a number of places where cooking and-and travel come together. I've been to Spain, I've been a couple of times to different places in France. Mostly I've been to different places in Italy, uh, and from the-the north to the south: Sicily, Puglia, Rome, Venice—various places like that, and each experience is really very different, and that's been something that-that I've, the education of learning about a country through its food is something I've found really fascinating. As Americans, I think we often have this impression that the food of a country is a single thing, defined by two or three sort of ingredients. We-we may think of Italian food, for example, as just spaghetti and meatballs, um, because that's kind of the way we were raised to think it's just one single thing. Well, it's not. It's the-the food of even of a country, which, Italy is not a very large country geographically, but the diversity of its food and the-the-the ingredients that different parts of, cooks in different parts of the country rely on, is-is vastly different, and learning about those differences—whether it's part of the country uses one kind of cheese, part of the country uses another kind of cheese, some parts of the country which are very rich in terms of having animals that they can use will have a lot of meat in the diet, other parts of the country that are, that are more impoverished don't have so much meat in the diet, some parts of the country use tomatoes in almost everything that they cook, um, versus another region of the country that doesn't—and just learning why the people in different parts of the country, um, use certain ingredients, don't use other ingredients and-and the wonderful things that they can make out of the simplest combination of ingredients is-is what I've really enjoyed learning about.

Well, as an example of sort of the simplicity of cooking, um, when I was in Rome once and-and on one of these cooking tours, um, I learned about a very simple pasta dish, which has nothing more in it than, um, a can of tuna and a little bit of oil, garlic. Garlic is an important ingredient in Italian food, um, which adds spice and complexity. Um, all of these ing—, simple ingredients—the-the tuna, some chili, red chili flakes, um, and the garlic—are cooked very briefly just to warm them up. Then you cook pasta, um, a, something like a spaghetti or a linguini kind of pasta, and while the pasta is still warm, right out of the water, you add it to this warm mixture of tuna and oil and garlic and chili flakes, and then you add to that some, a-a fresh green, um, something sort of spicy or bitter like arugula, or what, uh, what the British call rocket—I never quite understood why they use that different term, but they do—and the heat of-of the sauce and the heat of the, of the hot, fresh cooked pasta sort of wilts the green vegetable and it all comes together in just the simplest way. You add a little fresh lemon juice and that's it. It's just simplicity, but it's so simple that each of those ingredients in the dish contributes a special elegance and a special flavor to it, just all in itself. It's just wonderful—and quick and easy. But it-it reflects the, this desire that certainly the Italians have of using what's available to them, um, and emphasizing the individual ingredients, not clouding them with heavy sauces or things of that sort.

2. A WIDE RANGE

MAN: Good question. Uh, I like a wide range of foods from American to **Pakistinian**, Greek. Uh, I have a broad-broad taste when it comes to food. I don't do much, uh, unhealthy foods, though. I-I'm pretty serious about health, so I don't do too much fried foods and, um, I like to cook, so . . .

INTERVIEWER: So what-what's your favorite thing to cook? Can you, tell me about one of your favorite dishes?

MAN: Chicken.

INTERVIEWER: Chicken?

MAN: Yeah—there's no wrong way to cook it. There's so many things that you can do with it. But, um, I actually, uh, I like stewed chicken, you know, cut up onions, maybe some peas, carrots in the chicken. I like jasmine rice or yellow rice, chickpeas—oh, man—your-your broccoli, cheese sauce, things of that nature. Simple but, you know, real nice, healthy for you.

INTERVIEWER: What's your favorite ethnic food, other-other than food, uh, that's not an American dish?

MAN: My favorite. That's an interesting question, 'cause it's like comparing apples to oranges. I have several favorites, so it's **kinda** hard to pick.

INTERVIEWER: Pick one, any one.

MAN: One particular favorite. Ah. Tandoori chicken is one of my favorites, um, which is, uh, Pakistinian, Indian-style, and I like what they call samosas, uh. I have—**oh my gosh**, it's so much—I like curried okra. It's-it's so many different dishes, but I would say Indian dishes would be my favorite. Indian dishes. I would say the Tandoori chicken is probably one of my favorites or chicken masala.

INTERVIEWER: Are there any particular regional American foods that you like?

MAN: **C'mon**, hamburger and fries. You know, I do occasionally, you know, have my taste for junk food, so a **Fuddrucker** burger is not the worst thing to have. So occasionally I will **stop in**, I'll-I'll have a burger and-and some fries. That's-that's pretty much about it. I don't do too much other like junk kind of food, but that's-that's I guess about my-my favorite American dish.

3. MIDWESTERN COOKING

WOMAN: I love cooking, **I'm a big cook**.

INTERVIEWER: What kind, any type of food in particular?

WOMAN: No. I will, I like, whatever it is I like the taste of, then I want to learn how to do it. Um, I think, uh, it's a factor of growing up in the Midwest where in an, you know, Irish family where dinner consists of meat and potato. And seasoning is what, maybe salt and possibly ketchup? Um, and I remember when I went to college and, uh, started tasting all these other foods, I was like, "Oh my gosh, I've been missing out all this time! This is terrific!" Um, so yeah, anything that isn't bland, I'm a fan of.

4. NOODLES AND SAUSAGES

WOMAN: I-I like to eat a lot, so I-I have a broad range of what I like to eat. I, uh, I'm-I'm very fond of Taiwanese food, the food that I grew up with. I like, um, dumplings, I like spring rolls—the Taiwanese kind, not the fried American kind. I like lots of noodles, any noodle dishes that we have. Um, but ever since I was sixteen and went to France for the first time and stayed with a host family there, I'm a big fan of French food and Alsatian food in particular, so the Germanic heavy potatoes and sausage thing—I love sausages and potatoes, sauerkraut. I could eat that all day. Um, but pretty much I'll eat anything you throw at me. I-I-I really enjoy eating. It's one of the things that I, um, I love to do.

INTERVIEWER: Do you cook those things as well?

WOMAN: With limited success. It's always better if somebody else cooks it.

5. CAMEROONIAN CUISINE

MAN: I actually have a very simple, uh, approach to food. I know what I like and I don't try to deviate a lot from it. I like, once it has rice in it, I'm happy, you know, so, I love rice so you'll see me eating Chinese or rice cooked from the house or if I have to eat fast food, I eat **McDonald's**, you know. A lot people consider it fast food and so that's good, but I-I like McDonald's so I eat McDonald's and, uh, I know I have a high metabolic rate so I'm not too worried about, uh, eating from McDonald's.

INTERVIEWER: Do you cook for yourself a lot or . . . ?

MAN: My wife cooks a lot. Uh, I cook on intervals, uh . . . When I cook, it's an entire ceremony because I like to wear my hat, like a chef, have an apron and then cook about three dishes and so it's, uh. She always loves it when I cook that—it's always usually a surprise, by the time she returns from work and the chef has **done his thing**, you know. But she cooks on a daily basis.

INTERVIEWER: What's your best or favorite dish you cook?

MAN: Rice and stew.

INTERVIEWER: Really?

MAN: Yes. And stew is like a tomato base with, uh, like add a chicken or beef or gizzard or . . . So that's what we call stew but you have to have tomatoes, uh. That's what I have in common with the Italians, is the tomato, yes, and, of course, rice. And then we have *fufu* and *eru*, which is my traditional dish. Uh, a lot people in Cameroon, uh, love eating *fufu* and *eru*. It's very, very delicious. I just don't eat it on a regular basis as, uh, other people rather me do, you know. But, uh, I love *fufu* and *eru*, rice . . .

INTERVIEWER: What are in, what are in those dishes?

MAN: In *fufu* and *eru*? It's, um, it's a cassava-based, uh, substance. It's like, uh, I would compare the texture to mashed potato only a little denser, that's what a *fufu* is, so you usually eat it with your hands. And then the *eru* is a vegetable, um, they have to slice it in very thin, uh, layers and then cook it with spinach or water leaf, as we call it, and they use, uh, red oil. It's palm oil, not the-the vegetable oil. And this oil you can get from international stores, uh, and then cook it with whatever else—snails or beef or chicken or anything. But with snails, it's even more delicious.

6. COOKING IN GUYANA

INTERVIEWER: Do you cook Guyanese?

WOMAN: Yeah, mostly, yeah. . . . We are, we are, uh, in fact, sometimes we even call Guyana West Indian, I guess because of the British, um, influence. We speak English; we consider ourselves part of the West Indian culture, and that's what I cook mostly. In fact, that's what I, that's what we cook, West Indian food, mostly.

INTERVIEWER: So what-what are the main dishes that you cook?

WOMAN: Well, we have a thing called *pelau*, which is rice and chicken and pigeon peas. Uh, you-you cook that all up together and-and that's a main meal—you just have that with a salad.

INTERVIEWER: Uh-huh.

WOMAN: Then we have a Guyanese meal that you call pepper pot, which is all different kinds of meat together and you put in it something that we call *cassareep*, which is, um, the, you-you put the cassava out to dry and then you squeeze it.

INTERVIEWER: Uh-hmm.

WOMAN: Uh, and they make, the juice of that is called *cassareep*, if you leave it to ferment for a—I'm not sure how long but for a while—and that's what you use, and you put that in it and it, and it turns brown so it's a very, very brown meat, and you eat that with white rice or whatever. And, of course, you must have your fried plantains, ripe plantains, you must have fried ripe plantains. And curry is another one of our-our, um, our-our dishes, um, and you eat that with either rice or with, uh, something that we call *roti*, which looks like a, something like a pita bread, but just-just a little different but just like a pita bread.

7. FOOD PHASES

WOMAN: In general? Um, I'm not very picky with food. I basically like everything. Um, I'm not a big meat eater but, uh, other than that, I eat pretty much everything. I, uh, I go through phases. Sometimes I-I'm into Italian food, and then I go through a phase when I'm really like into Thai food or—I like Asian cuisine a lot. And I also like, like the Southwest food, like, um, Austin is a great place for food, um, because they have that **Tex-Mex** food, but it's very good. They have just wonderful, wonderful Mexican restaurants in Austin. And I also like, like, uh, I lived in Arizona for a few years when I went in gra—, when-when I was in grad school, and they have this, they call it this **Southwest fusion** cu-cuisine and it's just very, very sophisticated. It has aspects of just traditional **Southwest** food but kind of very innovative and very sophisticated and beautifully presented and I like that, too.

INTERVIEWER: How is food in-in general in America different from what you grew up with?

WOMAN: Well, um, I think that one of the things that I like about food in Spain is that it, uh, it incorporates a lot of fresh elements, so, you know, you have some dishes in Spain that are very elaborate, but like everyday food is actually very simple but, uh, people eat a lot of fresh fish, uh, you know, fresh vegetables, fresh fruits, and that's, eh, I think that's a nice thing about Spanish food. Like every day, what people eat at their houses, not necessarily what you eat when you go to a restaurant.

DEFINITIONS

'cause: Short for *because.*

c'mon: Common pronunciation of *come on.*

done his thing: To complete a job or task.

eye-opening: Suddenly enlightening or educational, or enlightening or educational in a way that significantly adds to or contradicts previously held concepts of knowledge.

Fuddrucker: An American fast-food chain.

I'm a big cook: *Big* in this sense means "enthusiastic."

kinda: Kind of.

McDonald's: An American fast-food chain.

Midwestern: Refers to the central portion of the United States.

oh my gosh: Common exclamation.

Pakistinian: Usually *Pakistani*; of or pertaining to Pakistan.

Southwest: Refers to the southwestern portion of the United States—often Arizona, New Mexico, and Texas.

Southwest fusion: Combination of the foods typically found in the southwestern portion of the United States.

stop in: To go to or patronize a business.

Tex-Mex: A combination of Texan and Mexican used in reference to a type of cuisine.

QUESTIONS AND EXERCISES

1. What kind of foods do these speakers like?

2. Which of these foods have you tried?

3. What's your favorite kind of food and why? What kind of food do you not like and why?

4. What role does food play in your life? Is it important?

5. Write the recipe for a dish that you cook.

6. Identify three words or phrases in this chapter that are new to you, and write a sentence with each one.

CHAPTER 10

SPORTS

In this chapter, interviewees talk about the role of sports in their lives.

1. MINOR LEAGUE BASEBALL

MAN: Um, I don't follow professional sports very much. I would much rather do just about any sport than watch just about any sport. Although last year I started going to, uh, **minor league** baseball games here in Frederick, the Frederick Keys. They're a, they're a **farm team** for the Baltimore Orioles and the stadium is-is very close by here, it's very inexpensive and you can sit right-right up close next to the action. It's-it's a very, very relaxed atmosphere.

WOMAN: It's great.

MAN: Yeah, it's a lot of fun—lot of fun.

WOMAN: He got me addicted enough that I actually now go see the Iowa Cubs when I'm in Iowa in the summer, and I call him at night and I, we talk about minor league baseball. It's great.

MAN: Yeah. I have a-a friend who's a hard-core sports fan—just about any kind of sport but especially baseball—and he's gotten me into doing the **box scores**, you know, and keeping track of the whole thing, and I've-I've sent him copies so that he can critique them and tell me how to do better next season.

2. SECOND BASEMAN

MAN: When I was a kid, I, uh, I, uh, um, I was essentially asthmatic, um, very **asthmatic**. I-I met a guy named Steve Wheaton—I think he was two-two years older when-when, me, than when I, when I was eight, he was ten—and he, we played baseball and, um, baseball became my life. Baseball still is ex—, uh, I, um, it, I was extremely good at baseball, uh, I still, uh, I shouldn't say I-I am, uh, now, of course, but I-I-I was even, uh, some **Detroit Tiger,** uh, **scout** was scouting a guy that, you know, poetically, uh, was on the same team I was at Providence College in, uh, um. I only found out through my brother—I was playing against this guy and-and, uh, I only found out from my brother, from the-the-the coach that-that Detroit Tiger fan, uh, scout, said, "That guy out there can do everything, but that guy is much too small." But that was all, I-I but-but that's how, I-I-I-I was good. And I loved it. I loved it, I loved it. I dropped it in college while ba-basically, um, I would say I was, I had a-a scholarship I had to keep. You lose, uh, sports is something that, um, sports, it can be all, it has to be all consuming. If you want to be a pro at baseball, if you want to be a pro at anything, and you guys may know this, if you want, you have to totally devote yourself. It's, a-a-a-a major league baseball player, they-they say athletes are dumb. They-they may not necessarily be dumb, but a lot, almost everything they have, if you want to make it to the pros, you've got to be 110 percent devoted. If you're not, you're not **gonna** make it.

INTERVIEWER: What position did you play?

MAN: Second base.

INTERVIEWER: Why?

MAN: Second, um, second base because, uh, um, I didn't have the arm. Later w-went to shortstop—certainly didn't have the arm for the outfield. I was quick. I-I did have the arm from second base to-to first base in double play, and-and I could cover the ground there, and-and usually, uh, the second baseman hits, traditionally, the, one of the-the-the shorter guys and-and usually a hothead. And-and I was.

You know, you know, uh, it's the old **McLuhan thing**. I-I-I almost do prefer the radio.

INTERVIEWER: Why?

MAN: Because-because you have to put more of yourself into it. You have to, you have to, uh, provide—you have to provide, you've been there, you have to provide the surroundings, plus I-I believe the radio announcers are, well, television, they-they are, well, it's a, it's a, television, look, it's a hot medium so, uh, they are more **laid back** about it. I mean, uh, uh, so it **winds up**: "The pitch," "Strike." Well. But-but in the radio, you got, you know, this, this, this, and this **'cause** they **gotta** keep—and they're good—they gotta keep it going. And, so I do f—, actually, a lot of times when the television is on, I will have the radio, um, with, uh, the-the-the sound off.

3. FOOTBALL **TRYOUTS**

MAN: I think it's gonna be kind of intimidating, seeing that, um, there's gonna be a lot of people there probably bigger than me, probably stronger than me, but I'm just gonna have to prove it, that I'm worth it for the team.

INTERVIEWER: Do you know what the routine is for **open tryouts**? Do they tell you what drills you're gonna have to do—what exercises—what you're gonna have to demonstrate?

MAN: Uh, I don't know at this point. I'm just hoping to go on luck right now. Um, hoping that they just give me some drills that I can actually just pass and hopefully make the **first cut**. And from there, we'll, I'll figure out where to go.

INTERVIEWER: Are you doing your own conditioning and training program to prepare for that?

MAN: Um, I'm using the tire shop mostly, as my conditioning. I lift the tires, try to build up my arms. Um, I'm constantly walking around fast, to keep my cardio up. Um, I ch—, I try to eat a lot of protein so I can keep my muscles strong—stuff like that.

INTERVIEWER: And, uh, and the wallyball?

MAN: Wallyball, yeah. It's mostly cardio and more physical, I guess you can say. And I do that every Thursday night.

4. WATCHING SPORTS

STUDENT: Yeah, I really like watching sports, uh, with my dad especially 'cause he's kind of a character and, um, it's kind of weird 'cause I-I probably watch more sports with my dad than my brother does, which isn't very normal. But, uh, we like to watch basketball. Right now, **March Madness**. Kind of excited 'cause I had Georgetown going pretty far, and, um, we-we shout and, uh, we get excited, and it's-it's really fun. We also watch football, always root for Penn State 'cause that's where my dad went, and last year they had a really good year, so that was fun. Um, sometimes we watch some crazy things, like, we watched rugby, we watch golf, which is actually more interesting than I would imagine but not interesting enough to watch the whole thing.

INTERVIEWER: Why do you say it's more interesting than one would imagine?

STUDENT: Well, golf is typically assumed to be a boring sport, just someone hitting the ball and it goes into the hole somewhere, hopefully, if they're any good. But it's more interesting now 'cause of Tiger Woods, and he's

kind of a **big deal**, and we like to see him win just 'cause it's more interesting when he does. Um, yeah, usually we watch the **eighteenth hole**.

INTERVIEWER: The eighteenth hole?

STUDENT: Yeah, that's pretty much it. My dad, we'll, we, uh, my dad has that complex where you have to switch around the channels all the time so, uh, we'll-we'll go back and forth but we'll-we'll really watch the eighteenth hole.

INTERVIEWER: Are there any non-American sports that you like?

STUDENT: Uh, soccer. Uh, World Cup, that was really fun. Um, that's really international. And then the Olympics—actually, I don't know, I really like other things more than the Olympics, but everyone plays there. Uh, rugby is international.

5. HOCKEY

WOMAN: Uh, I used to, I used to have season tickets with my dad, and I used to go to minor league hockey also with my dad when I was in Montreal. It's a lot harder to follow here, and since we work mostly nights, then never, can never watch the games so it's—I do, I do miss hockey.

INTERVIEWER: Did you play as you were coming up?

WOMAN: Yes. Yes. Oh, that was fun. That's actually a good story. Uh, I've always loved, you know, ice-skating. From the minute I could stand up, my dad bought me ice skates, of course, you know. And by the age of, like, four, uh, five or six, you know, I don't know if they have, like, girl hockey in the United States, but in Canada, you have, like, girl teams and guy teams, but the girl teams, the, it's-it's not a real hockey stick, it's just a stick with a ring, and basically you just, like, put the stick, you know, inside the ring and that's how you drag it on the ice, so it's not real hockey. It's weird. And basically, that's girl hockey, and I did not like that so after a couple of weeks of, like, playing that when I was five, I got really upset and I was, like, "Dad, I want to play with the guys. This is not hockey!" So my dad actually was able to, like, you know, put me in the, in the real hockey team with all the boys, and, you know, when you're five, it's OK, but by the time I was eight, some of the coaches and other boys and parents had issues about having, like, a girl in the locker room, so that's when I stopped playing hockey. But I did play real hockey for a couple of years as a kid. It was great.

6. A COMMON GROUND

MAN: I like to play 'em. I don't like to watch 'em too much, except for the playoff times but actually, I'm pretty athletic, uh.

INTERVIEWER: So what sports do you play?

MAN: Basketball, football, soccer, baseball—several of 'em, quite a few, quite a few sports.

INTERVIEWER: Are you in leagues or ⌈ do you just ⌉ pick up games or . . . ?

MAN: ⌊I used to be,⌋ I used to be, I used to play, um, high school ball, uh, played league balls around the community, um, street teams, uh, quite a bit of, a lot of trophies, medals through my youth, real athletic. I was a **PAL** boxing team. Uh, we train the children in self-defense also, which is, um, an important thing, try to teach them mental and physical discipline, so, yeah, I'm into sports. I-I like sports, yeah.

INTERVIEWER: What was your favorite sport?

MAN: Handball.

INTERVIEWER: Oh yeah?

MAN: Yeah.

INTERVIEWER: Why?

MAN: Oh man, what can't I say about handball? It's just a beautiful sport. It's hand-and-eye coordination, you, it builds and develops reflex, strength. It's-it's as good as swimming as far as, uh, muscle workout, you work out every muscle in the body. It's just, it's just an overall great sport.

INTERVIEWER: Uh, so you say you participate more than, you like to participate more than you like to watch. When you do watch, what sports do you like to watch?

MAN: I like to watch Ultimate Fighting Championships. I like basketball and-and football, and I tend to, I tend to watch those during playoffs and, but I will watch soccer. Soccer is something that, if I'm passing it, I-I kind of stop 'cause you have to admire the shape that these guys are in. We're talking about a field that's greater than the length of a football field. They're running forty-five minutes at a time, long periods before a break—the endurance involved in it is just incredible—so I like a good soccer game, and the fact that it's worldwide, it's not limited to any one particular region, so it crosses a lot of boundaries and-and it takes away, uh, a lot of the walls that are between people, you know, and-and it gives people a common ground. And that's one of the beauties of, beautiful things about sports, um, that it takes away the race barriers, it takes away a lot of the language barriers. It's just down to fundamental teamwork. You know the language of the game, you get there, and you do it. Everybody does their part, everybody doesn't have to score, everybody doesn't have to be the guy who runs the whole length of the game. You know, you just do your part. You might be the guy that just picks up for that superstar who gets tired. You give him a break so he can continue to be a superstar, the support team.

7. BASEBALL STRATEGY

MAN: To the casual observer, it takes forever and nothing really happens and it's not very interesting. Uh, but if you follow it and you kind of pay attention to the strategy that's going on, then it's an interesting mix of, uh, athleticism and that ability, but also, this mind game. And at its peak, you can sit there either watching the TV or watching a, at the game, and you can watch the mind game between the pitcher and the batter. Uh, we used to watch, and this is when—I laugh because this is when I knew my wife really had been totally hooked—when, uh, last year when Daryle Ward was, uh, playing first base a little bit with the **Nationals** and he was a, he was a batter that **fouled off** a lot of ba—, a lot of pitches, and you would just, you could, it was like watching a soap opera just for that **at bat**. You know, where the, what the pitch was gonna be, and he would **fight it off** and he'd kind of **stare down** the pitcher a little bit, and the pitcher would stare him down a little bit. It was just this great **mind game** that plays out in turns rather than all at once, so it kind of gives you that chance to sit back and watch it all unfold, um, rather than other sports like football or basketball that it's all kind of a **rush** and it happens right there. Uh, maybe I'd understand the strategy more if I knew more about those sports, but, uh, but that's what I love about baseball.

Uh, there's also this whole world of baseball, of the statistics, and people track this stuff and baseball is really known for, uh, for people being crazy with tracking all these **stats**. Uh, and, which actually, I, in a, in a kind of dumb way, and I can't believe I'm telling you this, but ties in a little with the Grateful Dead thing because people, you know, a lot of **Deadheads** will keep stats, you know, how many times you saw what song or what concert at, where, you know, what venue, and things like that, uh, and I remember meeting a guy at a show at Shoreline Amphitheatre in, uh, California, and he was, after the concert, and he was—we were sharing a hotel room and after the concert—he was noting down his little stats and I-I thought it was the funniest thing, because I did the same thing, but I had never realized other people did that. And I realized from talking, and from talking to him, we realized that we both also had this love of baseball and the statistics, uh, and he was a business statistics major, and we got into this whole conversation. And it was right at the time where I was switching from history to, uh, or from geoscience to history, and it kind of planted the seed of, uh, of-of using some of these same interests in a different setting.

The end, the end of the game, which is why I never understood people that leave in the seventh **inning**, 'cause that's, you know, it all builds up to, you know, unless they, unless it's twelve to one in the fifth inning and then it's **kinda** done but, uh, it-it all builds up to the strategy at the end, you know, towards the end, uh, and it-it, that-that's the best part. And I like sitting where you can see—I like now sitting behind home plate. My tickets are behind home plate but up. Uh, I like sitting behind so you can really see where the pitch is, um, and that's important. If you're sitting like out in the outfield, I think that's one reason why, you know, if you're kind of a casual fan and you get sort of the not, you know, the-the cheaper seats, uh, you can't really see so much of the stuff that **colors the game**, which is why I think sitting, you know, **dead center** at **RFK** is less exciting.

INTERVIEWER: Uh, if you could play, what position would you play and why?

MAN: If I could play. Uh, we used to play a game, one of, friend at work had a thing where if you could, during the Olympics, they would ask that, like, you know, if you could do any one sport in this, in the Olympics, you know, which would it be? Um, and I think I decided on, I think he had decided on moguls. I had decided on something else, I forget what. It was a skiing event, though. Uh, in baseball, if I could do one thing and why, uh, as a kid, I wanted to be a **pitcher**. And why, I don't know but it-it's just such a crazy, ridiculous thing to do or be good at, to take this little thing and make it move in unpredictable ways to try to get it past some other guy. Uh, it-it's, that's a, that's another aspect of baseball that I just think is-is so bizarre. Um, you know, the ball is so small and it just, you know, to throw it ninety feet and have it do these crazy things and have some guy with a bat trying to hit it is just such a bizarre thing, uh, and then something that, uh, some, you know, in a sport where, if you succeed slightly more than a quarter of the time, you're really good, is just, uh, I love that.

DEFINITIONS

asthmatic: Suffering from asthma, a respiratory ailment characterized by wheezing and difficulty breathing due to inflammation and constriction of air passages in the lungs.

at bat: When a baseball player stands ready to receive a pitch from the opposing pitcher.

big deal: A special or noteworthy event or occurrence.

box scores: In baseball, a play-by-play record of the progress of the game from inning to inning.

'cause: Short for *because*.

colors the game: To have an effect on the progress or various aspects of the game.

dead center: The exact middle of something.

Deadheads: Nickname for the fans of the band the Grateful Dead.

Detroit Tiger: A member of the professional baseball team the Detroit Tigers.

eighteenth hole: The last hole of a standard round of golf.

'em: Short for *them*.

farm team: In sports, a minor league or semiprofessional team that is used by a major league or professional team to develop its future players.

fight it off: In baseball, refers to the batter's effort to prevent being struck out or making an out in his confrontation with the pitcher.

first cut: A term commonly used in sports in the process of selecting team members that refers to the first round of eliminating those players who are not good enough, who are undesirable, or who do not meet the criteria to become a member of a team.

fouled off: A phrase used in baseball when the batter hits a pitch but the ball does not land in the "fair" part of the playing field.

gonna: Going to.

gotta: Common verbal utterance of *got to*, which means the same as *have to*.

inning: An interval of play in the game of baseball. A regulation game consists of nine innings.

kinda: Kind of.

laid back: An informal expression that means "relaxed or casual."

March Madness: In American collegiate basketball, a term that refers to the postseason NCAA tournament process that involves sixty-four teams. It usually takes place at the end of March or in early April.

McLuhan thing: A reference to Marshall McLuhan, a Canadian educator, philosopher, scholar, and communications theorist probably most well-known for his statement "The medium is the message."

mind game: Slang for the psychological competition that takes place between competitors.

minor league: In American sports, the level of teams below the major professional leagues. These minor leagues often serve as training and development venues for future major league players.

Nationals: Professional baseball club in the Washington, D.C., area.

open tryouts: Athletic auditions or a recruitment process in which prospective players are tested and display their skills in hopes of being selected to become members of a team. In open tryouts anyone can try out for the team in question, not just players who have been recruited by the team.

PAL: Police Athletic League.

pitcher: A position in baseball; the player who throws the ball to the batter.

RFK (Robert Fitzgerald Kennedy Memorial Stadium): A sports stadium in Washington, D.C., named for the former attorney general of the United States.

rush: A sense or feeling of excitement.

scout: In this context, an employee for a professional sports team whose job is to observe and assess the talent of players who might be recruited to play for the team.

stare down: To look at someone very intently for the purpose of trying to intimidate him or her.

stats: Short for *statistics*. Used in sports to refer to numerical data collected about players, teams, games, and things related to a particular sport.

tryouts: Athletic auditions or recruitment process in which prospective players are tested and display their skills in hopes of being selected to become members of a team.

winds up (wind up): In baseball, the motion that a pitcher goes through in preparation to make a pitch to a batter.

QUESTIONS AND EXERCISES

1. List the sports that these speakers watch and play and explain why they like them.

2. Compare the role of sports in the United States with their role in other countries.

3. Which sports do you like to play or watch and why?

4. Explain the rules of a sport that you play or watch.

5. Which sport would you like to try and why?

6. Identify three words or phrases in this chapter that are new to you, and write a sentence with each one.